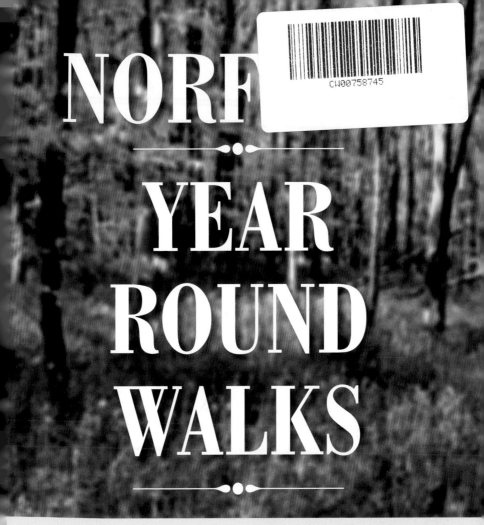

NORF

YEAR ROUND WALKS

Spring, Summer, Autumn & Winter

James Lowen

COUNTRYSIDE BOOKS
NEWBURY BERKSHIRE

COUNTRYSIDE BOOKS
3 Catherine Road
Newbury, Berkshire

To view our complete range of books please visit us at
www.countrysidebooks.co.uk

ISBN 978 1 84674 385 6

Photographs by James Lowen

All materials used in the manufacture of this book carry FSC certification

Produced by The Letterworks Ltd., Reading
Typeset by KT Designs, St Helens
Printed by Holywell Press, Oxford

Contents

Contents

Autumn

Winter

Introduction

With its big blue skies, open vistas and proudly slow pace of life, my adopted home county of Norfolk is ideally suited to a book that celebrates leisurely ambles rather than army-style yomps. The routes selected in this book revere the county's coastlines and its seductive saltmarshes, the sandy heaths of Breckland and the watery expanses of the Broads. There are walks through forest, fen and farmland that take in old ramparts and historical churches, remarkable windmills and wild nature reserves. Some ideas follow one or more of several long-distance footpaths that crochet the county; others take advantage of permissive walkways, serene country lanes or nature trails. Only uncompromising mountaineers can conceivably be disappointed with the strolls suggested – but everybody else should find the going rather easy, thanks to Norfolk's renowned flatness.

Across the walks collected here, I encourage you to visit well-known locations such as the royal estate of Sandringham – but also entice you to explore off the beaten track at such gems as Wheatfen. The selection can be enjoyed throughout the year, but I have sought to group them by the season in which I feel they particularly excel. Thus the bluebells of Foxley Wood is showcased in spring, the sandy seaside of Holme Dunes in summer, Horsey's coastal dunes and seal colony in autumn, and the wildness of The Wash estuary at Snettisham in winter.

All walks are circular and, in terms of distance, fall into the perfect post-prandial stroll spectrum of 2–7 miles. The routes are accompanied by simple sketch maps, which are designed to be used in conjunction with the relevant map in the OS Explorer series. Although many routes are accessible by bus or train, Norfolk does not have the most user-friendly public-transport network. I therefore assume that most readers will travel by car and thus offer directions and a parking place accordingly. As I firmly believe that all good walks should start or finish with sustenance, I recommend suitable watering holes or eateries near each route. Finally, to deepen your interest in what you are seeing, I suggest one or two things to particularly look out for as you stride. These vary from the static (think mills or other buildings) to the very much dynamic (silver-studded blue butterflies and kite-surfers), and from the seasonal (bluebells) to the scheduled (steam trains). There is something for everyone on each walk. Enjoy!

James Lowen

Acknowledgements

Sharon and Maya Lowen loved exploring several routes with me. Mick Davis and Ian Robinson kindly provided guidance on particular walks.

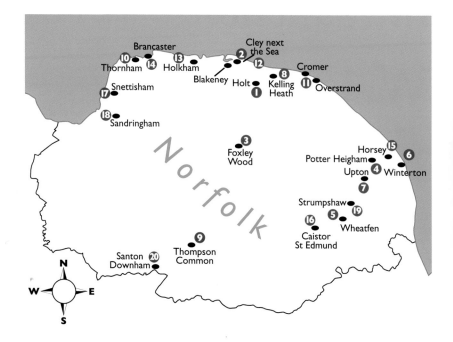

PUBLISHER'S NOTE

We hope that you obtain considerable enjoyment from this book; great care has been taken in its preparation. Although at the time of publication all routes followed public rights of way or permitted paths, diversion orders can be made and permissions withdrawn.

We cannot, of course, be held responsible for such diversion orders or any inaccuracies in the text which result from these or any other changes to the routes, nor any damage which might result from walkers trespassing on private property. We are anxious, though, that all the details covering the walks are kept up to date, and would therefore welcome information from readers which would be relevant to future editions.

The simple sketch maps that accompany the walks in this book are based on notes made by the author whilst surveying the routes on the ground. They are designed to show you how to reach the start and to point out the main features of the overall circuit, and they contain a progression of numbers that relate to the paragraphs of the text.

However, for the benefit of a proper map, we do recommend that you purchase the relevant Ordnance Survey sheet covering your walk. Ordnance Survey maps are widely available, especially through booksellers and local newsagents.

1 Holt Lowes and Country Park

2 miles / 3.3 km

A short but varied walk encompassing family-friendly woodland and wilder heathland and mire. Listen for firecrest and woodlark singing, admire buzzards floating in the air, investigate south-facing slopes for adders and watch common frogs or great crested newts in their breeding ponds.

Although the route largely follows very clear, signposted trails, the loop on Holt Lowes that explores the heathland pursues an undulating footpath that weaves between gorse bushes so needs a little more attention to stay on track. The rewards are worth it though. If you have a dog, please keep it on a lead – for the canine's sake as well as the snakes'!

The Walk _____

1 Make for the southern apex of the car park (diametrically opposite the visitor centre), behind which is a crossroads with the first of many coloured trail markers. Start by following the red trail, which curves south then east to reach a small pond. You arrive at a large pond, which is worth peering into, because great crested newts frequent the environs in spring.

NORFOLK *Year Round Walks*

spring

The Facts

Terrain Broad trails that are frequently muddy, and sandy or stony paths in the heathland. Rubber boots may be appropriate, depending on recent rainfall.

Map OS Explorer 251 Norfolk Coast Central.

Starting point Holt Country Park car park and visitor centre, off the B1149 Norwich Road, just south of Holt (GR TG 081375).

How to get there & parking Take the B1149 south from Holt. Just after you leave the town, ignore the turning to the right (west) towards Hunworth, and instead follow the B road south for 300 yards further, where the Country Park car park is signposted to the left (east). **Sat Nav:** NR25 6SP.

Refreshments The town of Holt has several options. My favourite is the outpost of Wells Deli, which serves monster Gloucester Old Spot sausage rolls among other hunger-sating treats ⊕ wellsdeli.co.uk. Better known is Byfords, which operates a café, takeaway and Posh B&B ⊕ byfords.org.uk.

2 Beyond the pond is a gate, which you pass through to reach the heathland of **Holt Lowes**. Turn left (north-east), climbing briefly up a stony slope to pass a wooden watchtower on your right (east). With the woodland to your left, continue north-east. Keep an eye out for adders. A good area to spot one is the area of dense gorse on your right 100 yards or so beyond the tower.

3 At a gate on the left (west), marked by two wooden statues of giants, the red trail ducks into the wood. Ignore this and continue following the blue trail north. The heathland opens out to your right (east). A path joins from the right (south-east); it has been shadowing you, unseen, 20 yards to your right

4 Where the blue path turns 90° left (north-west), two paths greet you to the right. Choose the nearest (southernmost) of the pair, and walk south-east on a loop to explore the heathland. The small path (a public footpath at this point, so marked on the OS Explorer map) heads gently downhill, then rises again as it weaves left, then right, then left again. Sandier now, the path heads south-east towards an obvious bank of tall trees. When you reach these, bear slightly left (due east) across a small stony area to reach an obvious path that heads north-east.

8

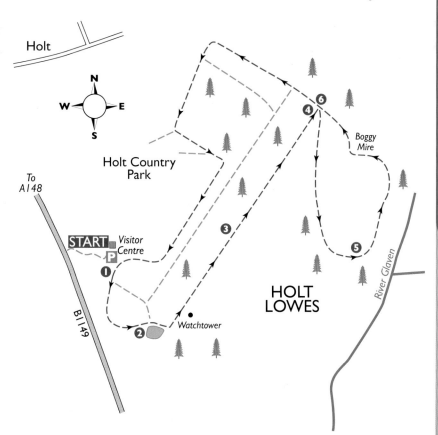

⑤ Follow this narrow but clear path as it weaves between gorse bushes. A sudden rustling at your feet probably signals a common lizard, but take care in case it is an adder. To your right, downslope, is birch-dominated woodland. The path curves gently round to the left, heading north-west. Here it passes an obvious boggy mire in the valley to the right, then dog-legs right (north) before curving back left (north-west). Keeping the woodland to your right, rejoin the blue trail at the point where you left it (step 4).

⑥ Head straight ahead, passing through the gate. Follow the blue trail as it heads left at the first junction, then right, then left again. It continues straight through the woodland for ⅓ mile (0.5 km) before eventually turning right to arrive at the car park. Along the way you should see forest birds such as marsh tit, goldcrest, great spotted woodpecker and nuthatch. Check any pathside ponds for breeding common frog (or ask at the visitor centre to discover where they are hanging out). If you have kids with you

spring

and you're looking for some more fun, there is a playground located just behind the visitor centre. This is another good spot for firecrest, and also neighbours a series of wooden sculptures and a sensory garden. There's plenty to occupy you at Holt.

What to look out for –

Adders

Confession time. I am what you might call 'addericted' to watching Britain's only venomous snakes. My location of choice for such serpentine observation is none other than the heathland at **Holt Lowes**. Male adders typically emerge from hibernation in late February. For the next few weeks, the 'boys' may gather in small groups, sharing body heat as they warm up in the sun. Once the somewhat tardier females have awoken and both sexes have moulted their skin, they turn their attention to breeding around mid-April. Males spar or 'dance' to exert territorial dominance, raising their upper body vertical and twisting their neck around one another in a hands-free wrestle. In theory, only the superior males win the race to procreate, but I have observed at least one subordinate male indulge in a sneaky mating while the 'alpha' male slumbered, oblivious to being cuckolded. By early May, libidinal activity is over for another year. For adders at least, spring has sprung.

2 *Blakeney, Cley and Wiveton Downs*

6 miles / 9.5 km

A quintessential north Norfolk coastal walk, but with a twist. As well as the unending skies, grazing marshes, saltmarsh-cosseted estuary and flint-rich villages, this route takes in one of the county's secret wonders: the narrow, winding ridge of Wiveton Downs. This glacial feature is England's finest example of an esker – a ridge formed by sand and gravel deposited by a river flowing through an ice sheet. Views from here are as good as from anywhere in the county.

You should see plenty of wildlife along the way. Mammals include hares and perhaps Chinese water deer on Blakeney Freshmarsh. Less wild, for sure, but certainly impressive are the longhorn cattle that graze Wiveton Downs reserve. Expect a transport hub of migrant birdlife – with brent geese feeding up before heading to the Arctic and yellow wagtails freshly arrived from Africa. On the lowland dry acid grassland of Wiveton Downs, look for spring butterflies such as green hairstreak among the gorse plus wild flowers such as native bluebells. It's enough to make you hungry – which is fortunate, as there is an abundance of fine eateries in this particularly 'foodie' part of Norfolk. It would be rude not to partake …

NORFOLK Year Round Walks

Terrain Hard-surface footpath along coast, country lanes inland plus a short stretch of rougher ground round Wiveton.

Map OS Explorer 251 Norfolk Coast Central.

Starting point Carnser car park at Blakeney Quay; National Trust members free, otherwise pay and display (GR TG 028442).

How to get there & parking From the A149 at Blakeney, take either Westgate Street or High Street a few hundred yards north to the quay, which is signposted from the main road. **Sat Nav:** NR25 7ND.

Refreshments An embarrassment of riches. In Cley next the Sea, barely 100 yards off-route are the fabulous delicatessen of Picnic Fayre ⊕ picnic-fayre.co.uk and Artemis Café, which offers amazing coffee and cakes ⊕ artemiscoffeeshop.co.uk. In Wiveton, the Wiveton Bell is a well-known gastro pub ⊕ wivetonbell.co.uk. On the A149, Wiveton Hall Café is highly rated – and even favoured by royalty ⊕ wivetonhall.co.uk. Blakeney Quay hosts a couple of takeaway huts providing good-value breakfasts and sandwiches.

The Walk

1 From the car park, climb the raised bank – part of local sea defences – to join the **Norfolk Coast Path** as it heads north. To your right is a pond with captive wildfowl; to your left the muddy channel departing the once-thriving port of Blakeney for the North Sea. Following the path north then east means you have saltmarsh to your left and the rough grassland of **Blakeney Freshmarsh** to your right. Skylarks sing overhead and newly arrived yellow wagtails may brighten the fields. On the tidal channel to your left (north), look for shockingly white little egrets (only a feature of Britain since the early 1990s) plus waders such as curlew and oystercatcher. Beyond is the shingle ridge of **Blakeney Point** – worth a yomp in its own right, as long as your legs can brave incessant shingle ('one step forward, two steps back' …).

2 As the Norfolk Coast Path veers back south, 1½ miles (2.5 km) from the start, **Cley Marshes reserve** opens up beyond the channel and road to your left (east). If visiting before May, you should see brent geese cackling as they nibble grass. Look out for marsh harrier and barn owl on both sides,

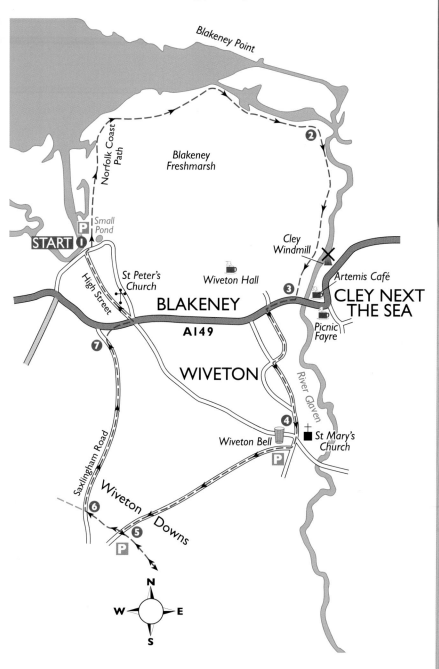

Blakeney Point

Norfolk Coast Path

Blakeney
Freshmarsh

2

Small
Pond

START **1**

Cley
Windmill

✕

St Peter's
Church

Wiveton Hall

Artemis Café

BLAKENEY

3

**CLEY NEXT
THE SEA**

High Street

A149

Picnic
Fayre

7

WIVETON

River Glaven

4

Saxlingham Road

Wiveton Bell

St Mary's
Church

6

Wiveton

5

Downs

N

W   E

S

spring

and timing your walk for the end of the day may enable you to encounter Chinese water deer. As you near the village of **Cley next the Sea**, with its eponymous windmill demanding your attention, reedbeds approach the path. Reed and sedge warblers sing here from mid-April onwards, while bearded tits and reed buntings are present year-round.

3 Follow the Norfolk Coast Path south until it reaches **Coast Road** (the A149). Rather than continuing left (east) into Cley (unless, of course, you fancy having a coffee or snack), descend the bank and turn right (west), along the A149 pavement for 150 yards to take the first left (south) towards Wiveton. Walk up this quiet, leafy lane to reach the cobblestone houses of **Wiveton village**. Turn left at the crossroads to reach another crossroads where the **Wiveton Bell** pub has a face-off with **St Mary's church**.

4 Go straight over at this crossroads (signposted to Holt and Glandford), then turn immediately right (south-west) along a narrow country lane, with the village car park on your left (south). Follow this gently rising lane, alongside which the hawthorn hedge should froth white in April and May, for ¾ mile (1.2 km).

5 Just before you reach the highest point, take a track to the left (south-east), signposted to **Wiveton Downs local nature reserve**. This leads to a car park, beyond which lies grassland, gorse-rich scrub and some obvious viewpoints. Avail yourself of these before returning to the car park, beyond which a kissing gate leads back onto the road. Straight ahead is another gate leading to the western portion of Wiveton Downs. Follow the permissive path along here, admiring the longhorn cattle that serve as a management tool to remove scrub, until it emerges at **Saxlingham Road**.

6 Descend this quiet, attractively open lane as it coaxes you just over ¾ mile (1.4 km) northwards to the outskirts of Blakeney village.

7 When you reach the A149, turn right (east) to walk along the pavement. Take the first left at **St Peter's Church**, to walk down **High Street** back to **Blakeney Quay car park**. If tides permit, there may be time in the day to join a boat trip to see the colony of harbour and grey seals at **Blakeney Point**.

spring

What to look out for –

Cley Windmill

The most eye-catching landmark along the walk is **Cley Windmill**, with its village-edge purview over the marshes and reedbeds towards the North Sea. Built in the early 19th century, the five-storey tower mill has been converted into a characterful guesthouse. Residents can walk around the mill on the second-floor stage, which puts you twenty feet above the ground; the views are brilliant! For more information and details on dining or staying at Cley Windmill, see ⊕ cleywindmill.co.uk.

3 Foxley Wood

3 miles / 4.8 km

This walk pays homage to one of Norfolk's most treasured woodlands, Foxley Wood. This sylvan gem – the county's largest remaining ancient forest – is a National Nature Reserve managed by the Norfolk Wildlife Trust. Paths chainmail between sunny coppices and dense woodland, opening up into orchid-strewn rides. In spring, the wood is full of birdsong, with marsh tits, willow warblers and garden warblers among the feathered stars. Arrive for dawn to experience the avian chorus at its most resonant. As additional reward, you will have the place to yourself.

There are so many paths through Foxley Wood that you could simply follow your whim, wandering at will. The suggested route, however, combines the best publicly accessible bluebell areas with some less frequented, more wild-feeling haunts. A lovely, leisurely and tranquil wander.

The Walk _____

1 Leave the car park along the entrance track in the direction you arrived (north-east), then turn right (south-east) along the first main ride. This is as expansive and sky-heavy as **Foxley Wood** gets, granting plenty of light should you wish to photograph the early purple orchids and water avens that splatter the verges with colour.

Terrain Mostly muddy paths, boggy in places. Rubber boots advisable.

Map OS Explorer 238 Dereham & Aylsham.

Starting point Norfolk Wildlife Trust car park at Foxley Wood reserve, Themelthorpe Road, between Foxley and Themelthorpe villages (GR TG 049229).

How to get there & parking Foxley Woods reserve is signposted off the A1067 between Lenwade and Guist. About 1¼ miles (2 km) north-west of Bawdeswell, you enter Foxley village. At the north end of the village, follow the signpost right (east) on Themelthorpe Road. Continue for 1¼ miles (2 km) until you see the car park signposted to the right, just after an isolated house. **Sat Nav:** NR20 4QR.

Refreshments The best bet locally is Hampton's in Bawdeswell ⊕ hamptonsatthebarn.co.uk; open 10–16h30 daily plus Friday evenings.

2 At the next junction turn left, entering a more heavily wooded area. Continue for 400 yards, ignoring various rides on both sides until the main path directs you right (signposted 'to the bluebells' in season). Access is often not permitted straight on, so you have to turn right anyway.

3 The wood becomes shadier and bluebells start to coat the floor, particularly when you reach a wooden bench dedicated to **Major General F. E. Ashenhurst**. Paths can be muddy here, particularly when peak bluebell season can see hundreds of visitors trampling the ground each day. Scenic rides full of bluebells traverse this path; take time to admire the plants from ground level.

4 As you reach another bench, the path turns 90° right (south-west), transforming into an open grassy ride, with a ditch furrowing away to your left (east). At a five-way junction, continue straight on, following the white arrow.

5 At a major crossroads, walk straight over the vehicular track which is the first main ride you walked along in step 1. Mature hazel coppice lies to your right (north). Listen for the plaintive sigh of a bullfinch, the

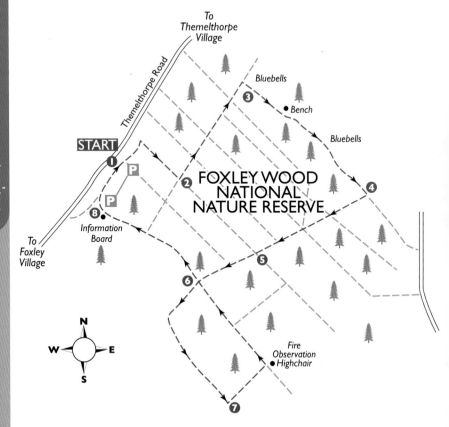

shimmering cadence of a willow warbler and the more limited refrain of the numerous chiffchaffs.

6 After 300 yards, you reach another crossroads at the woodland edge, with a field in front of you. Continue straight on, staying just inside the woodland on a narrow, sticky path. This is my favourite area at **Foxley** – away from the crowds, yet rich in a range of colourful wild flowers. It is a clandestine paradise that you have to yourself in exchange for getting your footwear a little muddy.

7 The path swings left at a trickle of a stream. When you reach a crossroads marked by an elevated 'chair' that serves as a fire observation point, turn left again. Continue straight on for ²/₃ mile (1 km), ignoring both the crossroads you passed in step 6 and the three subsequent junctions.

spring

8 At the fourth junction, signalled by a large information board, turn right to pass between two green-and-white metal poles. This brings you back to the car park, where you can rid your boots of mud before climbing into your vehicle, perhaps tired but certainly happy.

What to look out for –

Bluebells

Bluebells routinely crest polls of Britain's favourite flowers, and for just reason. In deciduous woodlands countrywide, the purple haze of April and May is eagerly awaited – and rarely disappoints. The Woodland Trust has identified some 1,500 forests worth visiting to see bluebells, so you have no need to travel far to experience them. In Norfolk you can do no better than admire the spectacle at **Foxley Wood**. Here the carpet of nodding 'bells levitates six inches above ground. Bluebells are the best, period.

4 Potter Heigham and Hickling Broad

5²/₃ miles / 9 km

A rich walk through some of the best of the Norfolk Broads, enabling you to thread through enticingly varied landscape comprising damp carr woodland and farmland, reedbeds and broad, river and grazing marsh. This route treats you to visiting Potter Heigham Marshes, perhaps the boldest venture yet from the Norfolk Wildlife Trust. A former grazing marsh between the River Thurne and Candle Dyke has been transformed into a new wetland habitat, designed to provide homes for bittern, marsh harrier and breeding waders such as lapwing.

The Walk

1 From a car park bordered with giant willows, head north-west along **Bridge Road** – away from the River Thurne – and turn right at the first crossroads along a public footpath that follows a farm track. Cross the A149 and continue through grazing marshes and damp fields for ²/₃ mile (1km) to the first junction.

2 Turn left (north-west) here, continuing along the uneven road after the footpath leaves it to the right (north-east) at a farmhouse. Continue roughly west along **Marsh Road**, passing a long series of houses to your

NORFOLK Year Round Walks

Terrain Stony farm tracks and sometimes muddy footpaths. Rubber boots useful after rain.

Map OS Explorer OL40 The Broads.

Starting point Car park opposite Latham's shop, Bridge Road, Potter Heigham (GR TG 419185).

How to get there & parking Potter Heigham lies off the A149, 5¾ miles (9.3 km) south-east of Stalham. Leave the A149 at the A1062 junction, heading south, then turn left (south-east) after 200 yards along Bridge Road. After ½ mile (0.8 km), use the car park opposite Latham's store ⊕ lathams-potter-heigham.co.uk. This is a pay-and-display car park. **Sat Nav:** NR29 5JD.

Refreshments Norfolk café chain Flour & Bean has a branch in Latham's ⊕ flourandbean.com. Next door BridgeStones offers classic British fare, and is usually busy ⊕ bridgestonesofpotter.co.uk.

left and two large farms to your right (including **Hall Farm**) until you reach the church of **St Nicholas** with its unusual round tower.

❸ Turn right here, keeping the churchyard to your right. After 200 yards, the road turns sharp left and a public footpath veers right (east) along a field edge. Follow this east then north, admiring butterflies that throng along the hedgerow to your right. After 300 yards, the footpath forks as it enters woodland. Follow the left branch, heading north through the shady, boggy terrain until you emerge at a small bridge over a channel. Cross this and climb the bank to reach the **Weavers' Way**.

❹ This 61 mile (98-km) footpath links the towns of Cromer and Great Yarmouth. Follow it east as it fringes the south-east corner of **Hickling Broad** then winds by **Heigham Sound** on its way south-east towards the River Thurne and thence into **Potter Heigham**. Reedbeds dominate the view to the left of the path, beyond which you catch occasional glimpses of open water and even yachts enjoying an aquatic excursion. Pause at the bird hide overlooking **Rush Hill scrape**, where lapwings may scurry and avocets lope. As you stroll steadily east then south-east, a variety of warblers will titillate your ears: sedge, reed and even grasshopper from the reedy areas, and blackcap, chiffchaff and willow warbler in the trees of **Sound Plantation** to your right (south). In the grazing marshes that

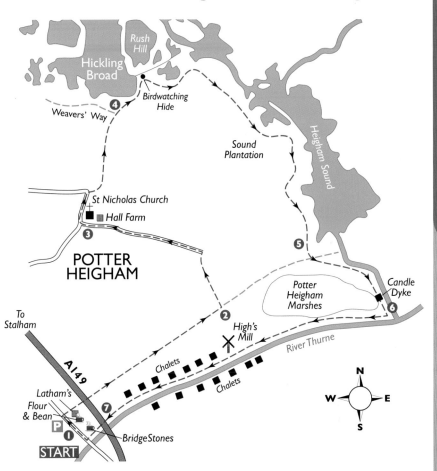

spring

culminate this step of the walk, look for yellow wagtails scurrying around the hooves of cattle.

⑤ The **Weavers' Way** descends from its embankment to join the easterly extension of the rough farm track that you walked along in step 1. In front of you is one of several scrapes (shallow lakes with muddy edges) that make up **Potter Heigham Marshes**. Follow the **Weavers' Way**/farm track south-east as it passes a cottage to rub shoulders with **Candle Dyke**, a channel that connects the River Thurne with Hickling Broad.

⑥ After ½ mile (0.8 km), you reach the bank of the **River Thurne**, a windmill to your left on the opposite side. Follow the **Weavers' Way** right (west-south-west) here for 1⅓ miles (2.2 km) until you reach the A149

road bridge at Potter Heigham. The first half of your route is dominated by the newly constructed scrapes and wetlands to your right (north). Look for breeding and migratory waders, and perhaps for scarcities such as spoonbill. After you pass **High's Mill** on the right, the main interest is provided by the chalets lining the River Thurne to your left. This is a popular stretch for pleasure boats, kayakers and paddleboarders.

7 As you pass under the A149 road bridge, you emerge at a popular area where tourists feed ducks and swans. Turn right here, and you will find the car park at **Latham's** directly ahead.

What to look out for –

Church of St Nicholas

This church has an idyllic setting on the outskirts of a sleepy village, far from the madding cry of the tourists around **Latham's** (where you park). This is generally acknowledged to be one of Norfolk's most attractive churches. The building as a whole dates back to the 12th century, and it has a 14th-century octagonal extension which is among Britain's best-preserved examples.

5 *Wheatfen*

2⅓ miles / 3.8 km

To walk through the Ted Ellis reserve at Wheatfen is to be privy to a Broadland secret. Accessed along a bumpy track from a small village and extending to one of the quieter parts of the River Yare, Wheatfen feels very far indeed from the madd(en)ing crowd of the tourist Broads. Wheatfen's trails are blissfully quiet – this reserve is the domain only of the lucky (and in-the-know) few. Established in honour of famous Norfolk broadcaster and naturalist Ted Ellis, Wheatfen is one of the few remaining areas of the once-extensive Yare Valley swamp. Managed by a small, independent charity, the reserve's landscape mosaic blends damp fen with reedbed, and sallow carr with open broad – all masticated by the daily ebb and flow of the Yare itself.

From mid-April Wheatfen resounds to the libidinal serenades of various warblers. Male cuckoos plaintively seek a mate who may choose to rob those same warblers of their offspring. Marsh harriers coast overhead, scouring the reeds for inattentive voles or rodents. A sunny day late in spring should see a riot of dragonflies and damselflies.

Terrain Short section of boardwalk, then often muddy or grassy trails through the reserve, which can be boggy in places. Rubber boots usually advisable.

Map OS Explorer OL40 The Broads.

Starting point Ted Ellis reserve car park at Wheatfen, The Covey, off The Green, Surlingham (GR TG 325056; 🌐 wheatfen.org).

How to get there & parking From the A47 south of Norwich, turn south on to the A146, then turn left (north) at the first set of traffic lights, where the B1332 comes in from the right (south). Follow the minor road as it curves east. At the Y junction in Bramerton, turn left (north) onto Surlingham Road. Keep along the 'main' road through Surlingham village. After you pass the school, garage and post office, turn left (east) off Mill Road onto The Green. At the T junction, turn right (south) driving along an increasingly rough track for ½ mile (0.8 km) until you reach the reserve car park on the left. **Sat Nav:** NR14 7AL.

Refreshments North-east of Surlingham village on the River Yare, situated along a narrow road east of The Street is Coldham Hall, a smart pub that offers an inventive menu starring local produce 🌐 coldhamhalltavern.co.uk.

The Facts

The Walk

❶ From the car park, head straight on (east-north-east), past **Wheatfen Cottage**, the home of the Ellis family since the end of World War II. Turn left (north) over the bridge at **Home Dyke** (an old peat digging), pausing to digest the information board, before continuing along the boardwalk.

❷ Emerging from a short stretch of carr woodland, you pass a thatched bird hide ('**The Thatch**') adjacent to a small pond that often heaves with dragonflies. The boardwalk now relinquishes duties to the often-muddy paths and rides that you will follow for the rest of the walk. As you walk north, **Old Mill Marsh** lies to your right (east). It is mown each winter to encourage floral diversity. At the junction of paths, bear left, then turn immediately right through a lightly wooded area.

❸ The path now turns almost 90° right (east-north-east), bisecting tall

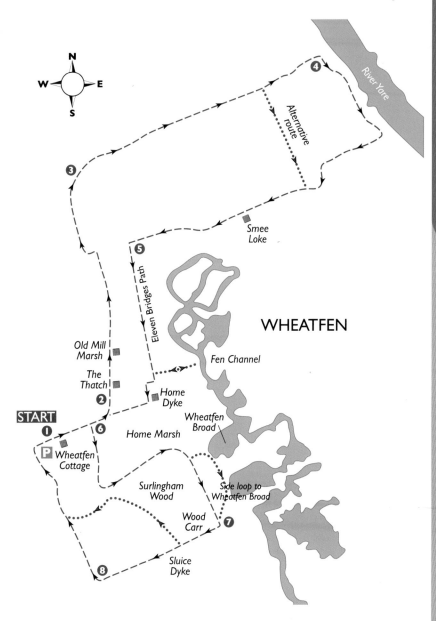

fen. On sunny days, pathside vegetation (even nettles) throng with insect life. This stretch is famous among bug-hunters for being the only place in the country where a small, bronze beetle (known only by the scientific name of *Galeruca laticollis*) occurs – although you are unlikely to see it

until mid-summer. This is also a good sector to hear reed, sedge and grasshopper warblers, to watch scarce chaser and other dragonflies, and to spot a marsh harrier soaring over.

4 In spring and summer, the path extends north-east to greet the **River Yare** then heaves to the right (south-east) for 200 yards, before turning sharp right again to lead broadly south-west. This is **Smee Loke**, which runs for ⅓ mile (0.5 km). Here a rich flora includes ragged robin and hemp agrimony, attracting a raft of colourful butterflies. Depending on the timing of your visit, you may see brimstone, peacock, small tortoiseshell or red admiral.

5 About 50 yards shy of the junction with the path you took on the way out, turn left (south) along **Eleven Bridges** path, which runs alongside a dyke. It may be hard to believe it this far inland, but this channel is tidal. Ignore the small path on the left (or explore it if you will; it leads along **Penguin Dyke** to **Fen Channel**), following the main path right then left across a bridge. (If you reach The Thatch, you've gone too far.)

6 Follow this path roughly south past **Home Marsh**, then east alongside **Surlingham Wood**. If it is open, follow the side loop left (east) to garner views over **Wheatfen Broad**. If it is closed, continue straight along the main path.

7 The small loop rejoins the main path, where you turn left then cross the bridge into **Wood Carr**. At the end of **Sluice Dyke**, cross the bridge and head right (roughly north).

8 The final section of the wood is noticeably drier underfoot, which may be a relief. Continue for 300 yards to rejoin the car park.

What to look out for –

Swallowtail

A lemon flash heralds the arrival of the Norfolk Broad's most famous animal. Looping around and over your expectant head, the swallowtail alights on a favoured plant. It continues to rapidly flap wings of lacy lingerie so as to maintain a position conducive for unfurling its proboscis ('tongue') and slurp nectar. The adult butterflies emerge by late May and delight visitors on sunny days until July.

6 Winterton Dunes

4¾ miles / 7.5 km

Blow away the cobwebs with a varied walk that encompasses the sandy heath of Winterton Dunes National Nature Reserve plus nearby woodland and farmland. Along the route you can also pay homage to one of Britain's first offshore wind farms and sneak a peek at the quieter side of village life. The route starts at the beach (where grey seals are a common sight and little terns may fish offshore). It then chooses to head inland first, passing the outskirts of Winterton village. It cuts inland past a stately home and ruined church before traversing arable fields, rough pasture and woodland. Saving the best for last, you emerge from the trees onto the sand dunes of the National Nature Reserve.

The Walk

1 At the car park, first look out to sea. Admire the **Blood Hill wind turbines** that were among the first in Britain to generate carbon-free electricity. Then walk inland (west) along **Beach Road**, past the toilet block towards the village. To your left, atop a small hill, are small, circular 'Hobbit houses' – each brightly coloured with a conical thatched roof – that are holiday lets.

2 Just before you reach the first houses on the right, take the footpath that runs north in front of their gardens. At the end of this row of

Terrain Split broadly evenly between firm terrain (occasionally muddy) and soft, sandy ground.

Map OS Explorer OL40 The Broads.

Starting point Beach Road car park (seasonal charges) at the east end of Winterton-on-Sea village (GR TG 499198).

How to get there & parking Leave the A149 at Martham, heading east into that village, following signs for West Somerton. In that village, turn right at the junction by The Lion pub. Pass through East Somerton. When you reach Winterton-on-Sea turn left (east) onto Black Street which leads into Beach Road. The car park is at the end, on the left. **Sat Nav:** NR29 4DD.

Refreshments By the car park is Dunes Café, which offers a changing menu and is open from spring to autumn. ⊕ dunescafe.weebly.com.

dwellings, you meet a path that enters from the right (east). Follow this left (west), as it runs between houses and merges into **Low Road**. This 'road' deteriorates, eventually becoming a restricted byway. You pass paddocks on the right and a secluded public garden called **Duffles Pond** on the left, beyond which lie allotments and **St Cecilia's church**, whose rectangular spire protrudes above the greenery.

❸ Continue along **Low Road**, a hedge to your right and a group of holiday cottages to your left. The byway turns to tarmac when it joins **Manor Farm Road**. Bending right then left, the road passes **Manor Farm** and its attractive pond. Now named **Back Road**, it enters woodland where the ruins of **St Mary's church** persist to your left (south). Wrapped in creepers and interspersed with trees, this is an example of Nature reasserting its claim to the land. Beyond the church, you pass a high brick wall that ensures the privacy of **Burnley Hall**, a large Georgian property with towering chimneys.

❹ Just after the Hall, you reach a T-junction, where you turn right onto **Honeypot Lane**. An attractive thatched cottage marks a sharp left turn. Three hundred yards on, another footpath joins from the left at the apex of a woodlot. Ignore this, and follow the asphalt of **Holmes Road** right (north). Flanked by arable fields and rough grazing, continue north for

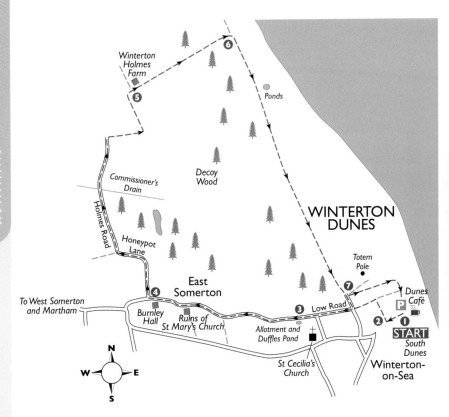

nearly 1 mile (1.5 km), crossing or running parallel with several drainage ditches, including **Commissioner's Drain**. Continue along the hedge-bordered road, which bends sharply right then left between fields, until you reach the barns of **Winterton Holmes farm**.

5 Cross the concrete pad in front of the barns and continue along the drivable track heading roughly north-east. After ½ mile (0.8 km), the fields become scrubbier and then you enter attractive deciduous woodland, where various warblers sing. On warm days, the shade provides welcome solace.

6 Emerging from the woodland at a gate, an information board announces your arrival at **Winterton Dunes National Nature Reserve**. Scattered concrete blocks served as defences during World War II. The natural scenery could hardly be more different to what you have seen

thus far in the walk. Sweeping, well-vegetated sand dunes are interspersed with lichen-rich hummocks that crunch underfoot, swathes of stunted bell heather and the odd shallow pond. The signposted footpath heads south-south-east, with a fence to your right (west), beyond which lies the private **South Wood** and, beyond that, the equally private **Decoy Wood** (named after a 19th-century duck decoy). To your left lies the dune heath. The formal route (as on the map) follows this footpath back to **Winterton village**, but you should feel free to wander instead along the tiny paths criss-crossing the dunes. These bring you to fenced-off ponds where natterjack toads and dragonflies breed (GR TG 487214), tracts of scrub favoured by cuckoo, stonechat and yellowhammer (as well as adder, so watch your tread), and to an odd wooden structure known locally as the 'totem pole' (GR TG 495199) and apparently linked to World War II communications. Alternatively, you could stroll south-east along the beach – but please avoid areas that have been roped off to protect nesting ringed plover and little tern.

⑦ Assuming you follow the main drag at the western edge of the dunes, continue south to the north-east edge of **Winterton-on-Sea** village. When you reach a grey building with blue metal shutters, turn left (east) to follow the public footpath (signed 'Winterton Dunes circular walk'). This takes you to beach huts that mark the northern edge of the car park. If you have too much energy left to call it a day (or if you are rejuvenated following lunch at the Dunes Café), you could do worse than cross the road into the South Dunes and explore these at will.

What to look out for –

St Mary's Church

Perhaps Norfolk's most dramatic ruined church, most people do not notice **St Mary's** until they are actually upon it – so boldly has plantlife reclaimed it. Built in the 15th century and discarded by the 17th century, only the nave, tower and chancel arch remain, the latter yawning an invitation for you to enter. Oaks and beeches shoulder the church walls – one of the former even flourishing in the middle of the nave – while ivy and elder coat the remaining brickwork with green. The result is serene, verdant, shady and powerfully natural.

Upton Broad and Fen

5 miles / 8.0 km

A taste of the Broads in summer, but off the beaten track. The fen at Upton Broad and Marshes reserve, run by the Norfolk Wildlife Trust, is one of the best preserved in East Anglia. In summer, it buzzes with swallowtail butterflies and Norfolk hawker dragonflies. Colourful orchids splatter a meadow that abounds with ragged robin – a pink plant that looks to have been formed by the erratic cuts of Edward Scissorhands. Warblers provide the soundscape as you stroll abreast the woodland. Meanwhile, this stretch of the River Bure boasts some of the county's most striking wind- and watermills – and that is saying something in a county where mills rule. But the very best thing? You are unlikely to encounter a single other person along the public rights of way and permissive footpaths.

The Walk

① Leave the reserve car park east, passing through the trees and past dense sedges to emerge in **Upton Fen**, a relatively open area from which four paths ply in different directions. Select the third path from the left. This cuts through reeds and past a couple of small pools. After 50 yards, you

Terrain Mainly grassy paths that are often boggy. Occasional short boardwalks. Rubber boots recommended after rain.

Map OS Explorer OL40 The Broads.

Starting point Norfolk Wildlife Trust reserve car park, Low Road, Pilson Green (GR TG 380137).

How to get there & parking Leave the A47 about 2 miles (3.2 km) west of the town of Acle. Head north-west on the B1140. After ¾ mile (1.2 km), turn right (north-east) along Green Lane. Bear left at the first junction, joining Acle Road briefly, then right at the second, onto Mill Road. Ignore the next junction (with Upton Road) and go straight over at the second junction. The reserve car park is on the right (east) after 150 yards. **Sat Nav:** NR13 6EQ.

Refreshments Two nearby pubs stand out: The Ship in South Walsham ⊕ shipsouthwalsham.co.uk and The White Horse in Upton ⊕ whitehorseupton.com. The latter has the advantage of being only a few hundred yards off route, whereas the former requires a short drive (but is worth it!).

reach a T junction. In front of you is a glorious damp meadow which, in summer, is rich in buttercups, ragged robin and southern marsh orchids. Then turn left (east) and continue for 250 yards, enjoying the sensation of bouncing along the distinctly spongy path – the legacy of a peat underlay – to pass through increasingly wooded terrain.

② At the fork, turn left and follow the path into an area of short vegetation with a small, isolated reedbed. This is another great area for orchids. Follow the path straight on, bearing left over a bridge. Off to your right, along a little path, is a viewing platform which you may feel merits a diversion to get a view of **Upton Broad**. Otherwise continue along the muddy path, using the planks to minimise disturbance to this fragile habitat, with a strip of carr woodland to your left. At a T junction, bear left on a wide path bisecting an area of tall fen. This stretch can be seriously boggy so watch your step. Stay left at the next two junctions, then cross a boardwalk to walk parallel to a ditch for 70 yards until you reach a slightly elevated permissive path than runs roughly west–east.

③ Turn right (east) here, following the blue posts marking the broad

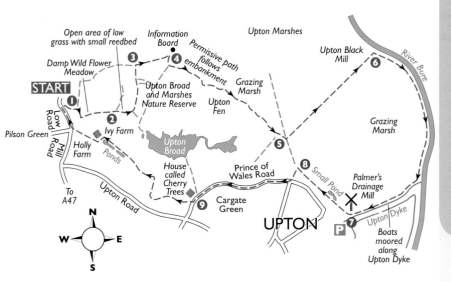

path that runs through a gate. To your left (north) a channel separates you from a reedbed frequented by marsh harriers. To your right (south), a stretch of sedge is favoured by dragonflies and damselflies. Forty yards after a lone hawthorn on your left (north), you cross another gate to reach a T junction. Before you unfolds a sizeable expanse of rough grassland, grazed by cattle. Beyond lie your first windmills and, further still, the crests of yachts hinting at the presence of the **River Bure**.

④ Twenty yards to your left an information board summarises the history of the area. Have a look then turn round and follow the permissive path that leads south then east. Water soldier – a spiky plant beloved of the Norfolk hawker dragonfly – crowds the ditch to your left (east), between you and the grazing marshes. To your right, beyond the herb border where yet more damselflies billow, lies carr so dense that it grants only the occasional glimpse of **Upton Fen**. Continue for ¾ mile (1.2 km) until you reach some tall willows.

⑤ A blue marker seeks to usher you along the public footpath to the right (south). Resist the temptation, instead bearing left over a bridge, past a pond to reach a concrete public footpath. Turn left then immediately right onto a stony vehicular track (also a public footpath) that leads north-east for ²/₃ mile to **Upton Black Mill**.

⑥ This impressive windmill and adjacent outhouses are worth a look – even more so because they front onto the **River Bure**, which is narrow and

sedate here. Then turn right along the footpath flanking the **River Bure**, with rough grassland to your right (south). Continue for just over a mile (1.8 km) as the riverside path loops gradually round to the south-west. Along the way you pass a mill on the opposite bank and, as you approach the village of **Upton**, a long series of boats moored along **Upton Dyke**.

⑦ Rather than enter the village, turn right (north-west) along a public footpath that passes **Palmer's Drainage Mill** (to your right). Continue alongside a belt of trees for ⅓ mile (0.6 km) until you cross a bridge and reach a T junction.

⑧ Turn left (south-west) here and walk 80 yards to join **Prince of Wales Road**. Turn right (west) and follow this quiet road out of the village and through fields until you reach the hamlet of **Cargate Green**.

⑨ Look for the house called **Cherry Trees** on your right (west). Between this and the following house, a vehicular track leads right (west) off the road. This is a public footpath. Turn down here, following it through fields to a T junction, where you turn right (north). At the next T junction, by a bridge, you turn left (west) and continue along the footpath. Just after two narrow ponds, the path jinks left to join a vehicular track that serves **Ivy** and **Holly farms** before joining **Low Road**. Continue along the road for 150 yards to reach the car park.

What to look out for –

Upton Black Mill

Surely no English county has a greater affinity for (water- or wind-) mills than Norfolk? The intimacy of the relationship is surely borne out of landscape – or, rather, waterscape. **Upton Black Mill** was a drainage mill, whose purpose was water removal. Although built of red brick (in 1800, judging from the date stone set under a window facing the River Bure), it was covered in black tar – hence its name.

8 Kelling Heath

3 miles / 4.8 km

A heady walk amidst swathes of lilac heathland stippled with silver birch trees. As the local steam train chunters past (a journey aboard makes a fun complement to this walk ⊕ nnrailway.co.uk), your vista north hints at the sea. Although there is free access over the whole of Kelling Heath, sticking to paths is more respectful of its rare avian and reptilian denizens. Even so, there are a myriad of paths to choose from, and the route suggested here may be bettered over time as the heathland matures in some places or, in others, is razed back to bare ground through careful management.

The Walk

1 Go through the gate at the north end of the car park, and head straight on (north-north-east). After 60 yards you pass through some trees, then emerge with an area of heather to your left (north-west), before trees return on that side.

2 At the first fork, stay right through a copse. At the second fork, beyond the information board, where **Plumpudding Lane** heads left (north-west), again bear left to continue north-east. Keep going straight along an obvious sandy path through the heather. The path penetrates a small copse then emerges into an open area as it morphs into an old cart track.

The Facts

Terrain Sandy paths, with occasionally muddy parts. Stout shoes recommended.

Map OS Explorer 251 Norfolk Coast Central.

Starting point Kelling Heath car park, Holgate Hill, ¹/₃ mile (0.6 km) north-east of Holt Garden Centre (GR TG 099417).

How to get there & parking Leave Holt east on the A148. Just after the hospital (on the left/north), turn left (north-west) at a staggered crossroads. Go over the railway bridge and turn right (north-east) at the first crossroads (known locally as 'Kelling Triangle') onto Holgate Hill. Pass Holt Garden Centre on your right (east). After ¹/₃ mile (0.6 km), look for a car park hidden down a stony track to the left (north). **Sat Nav:** NR25 7ER.

Refreshments In Weybourne, The Village Store is an excellent deli ⊕ tideaway.org.uk/the-village-store and The Ship, a decent pub whose menu is particularly sensitive to those with gluten- and dairy-free needs ⊕ theshipinnweybourne.com. Alternatively, try the suggestions in Holt (page 8).

❸ At the T junction, you will eventually go right (south-east), but before doing so, bear left (west) for 30 yards to a triangle of paths then right (north) to the viewpoint atop **Telegraph Hill**, which proffers a vista north down **Muckleburgh Hill** and to the glittering sea beyond. Return to the T junction and walk south-east, passing another viewpoint/bench on the left, which has a more easterly aspect towards **Weybourne** village and the town of **Sheringham**.

❹ Thirty yards beyond the bench, veer right at the fork. You now walk through 150 yards of heather, before turning slightly right (south-west) at an indistinct crossroads of paths. This leads through more stunning heather. After 60 yards, this path joins a broad old vehicle track. If you haven't yet spotted a silver-studded blue butterfly, you should do so now – for this area houses a colony. Follow this track south-west for 150 yards until it meets a triangle of gorse. Follow the path right here, reaching the end of the gorse after 70 yards.

❺ Here you hit another path, so turn left and follow it south-east to the road (**Holgate Hill**). Turn left and walk roughly north-east along the road for 300 yards until you reach the far (north) edge of the woodland. Join the public footpath, turning right (south-east) and continuing as the footpath reaches the railway line and is forced right (south-west).

6 Here the path flanks the railway, heading south-west to a house by gates that allow you to cross the line. If you can hear the local steam train coming, why not wait for it to pass so you can admire it? Then cross the railway line carefully.

7 Once across, walk straight on (south-east) for 300 yards – through an area that can be great for adder sightings – until you hit a belt of trees. The public footpath continues straight here (running past the southern edge of **Kelling Heath Holiday Park**). You, however, turn sharp left (north-north-east), keeping the heathland to your left and a belt of trees to your right. Continue straight for ⅓ mile (0.5 km) until you reach a T junction by a display board.

8 Turn sharply left (south-west) to follow the broad sandy track along the embankment above the east side of the railway line. When you reach the gates over the railway line (step 7), cross back to the west side.

9 Now head straight (north-west) along the largely sandy path until you reach **Holgate Hill** after 400 yards. Cross the road, then take the narrow path to the left, which winds through gorse and beside heathland as it returns to the car park.

What to look out for –

Silver-studded blue

This small, attractive butterfly is mainly restricted to lowland heathland and has become pretty rare of late. It went extinct on Kelling Heath in the 1970s, but a reintroduction programme in 2001 has proved very successful. Initially released at just two sites on the Heath, seven discrete colonies have now formed. See silver-studded blues on the wing between June and August.

9 Thompson Common

5²/₃ **miles / 9 km**

The Brecks (or Breckland) are probably Norfolk's most unusual landscape. With stunted, sandy grassland in a peculiarly arid micro-climate, the Brecks at Thompson Common hide a curious landform. Pingos are shallow, usually water-filled depressions that formed during the last Ice Age and now throng with dragonflies. Although common in the tundra of Alaska or Norway, they are almost unknown in Britain.

The route follows parts of both the Great Eastern Pingo Trail and the Peddars Way, Norfolk's premier long-distance footpaths. It traverses damp woodland carr, flanks quintessential Breckland grassland, rubs shoulders with a series of pingos and pauses at Thompson Water, a shallow lake created by damming the River Wissey during the 19th century.

The Walk

1 Follow the Pingo Trail through the gate at the south end of the car park, passing the former railway station at **Stow Bedon**, which last served trains in 1965. Heading south-south-west, the broad path – the old railway embankment – is slightly raised. Woodland birds chatter from birches to your right; hares and roe deer forage in fields to your left.

2 After a mile (1.6 km) you reach a junction with a drivable track. Here the **Pingo Trail** continues straight on. Forsake this, turning right (west-south-west) along the farm track, passing houses and **Crowes Farm** on your right. After **Heath Cottage**, ignore the sign for Cullinghurst Stud to your right, instead continuing straight on, past a metal barrier, along a

Terrain Easy flat walking. The terrain can be a little muddy or damp, so stout shoes or rubber boots are advisable.

Map OS Explorer 229 Thetford Forest in the Brecks.

Starting point Great Eastern Pingo Trail car park, off the A1075 Watton Road, near Stow Bedon (GR TL 940965).

How to get there & parking Leave the town of Watton south along the A1075. After 4 miles (6 km), just before Stow Bedon, look for a lay-by on the right as the road bears left. Turn into the lay-by and follow the track for a few yards to the car park on the right. **Sat Nav:** NR17 1DP.

Refreshments In Thompson village, The Chequers Inn is a thatched, 17th-century pub serving pub grub and offering rooms. ⊕ thompsonchequers.co.uk.

Forestry Commission path. Beech trees nuzzle both sides of the path, behind which lies a pine plantation.

③ After ²/₃ mile (1 km), a vehicular track crosses the path. To your left is an open area, to your right a wide ride through pines. Continue straight; the path becomes sandy and cosseted by ferns. Three hundred yards on (0.3 km), cross another metal barrier to join a road. Head straight, with a pig farm to your right.

④ Shortly afterwards, you reach a T-junction with the **Peddars Way**. Turn right (north-west) along the undulating, sandy path, with sheep-grazed **Breckland** grassland (a military training area, with no access) to your left. On your right a large standing stone is one of five sculptures by Tom Perkins that form the 'Norfolk Songline' project. Pause to read the inscription before continuing.

⑤ Re-enter the woodland to reach a viewpoint over **Thompson Water**. Scan this man-made lake for waterbirds such as gadwall and little grebe, and dragonflies such as migrant hawker, which patrol the air above the spiky aquatic vegetation known as water soldier.

⑥ After ¼ mile (400 yards), at the sign for **Stow Bedon** station, leave the **Peddars Way** by turning right (east-north-east) to rejoin the **Pingo**

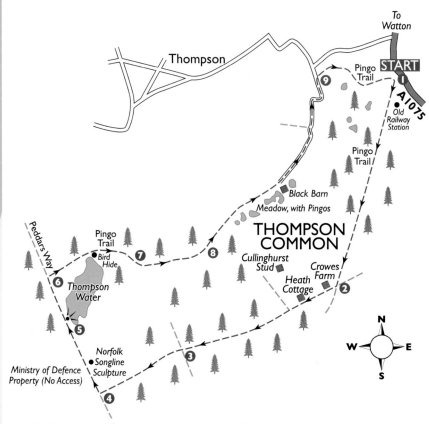

Trail. Here you enter the Norfolk Wildlife Trust reserve of **Thompson Common**, marked by a gate. The narrow path weaves through the forest, passing a simple wooden bird hide that offers views over **Thompson Water**. Continue past a couple of pingos on your left until you reach a signpost that is partly concealed behind a holly tree. Ignore the path that goes straight on, instead following the **Pingo Trail** arrow to the right.

7 Traverse coppiced hazel woodland where the ground can be a little boggy. At a bridge over a stream, turn left and walk parallel to the channel.

8 Crossing another bridge, you emerge into **Thompson Common meadow**. Exit the meadow through a gate. Fifty metres on, the path forks. Veer right; to your right, beyond a hedge, a grassy area conceals further pingos. At a black barn, the path merges into a tarmac road. Continue straight (north-east) for ⅔ mile (1 km), ignoring the sign for a public footpath to your left and passing several houses and a paddock.

⑨ Before you reach **Thompson** village, just before a Give Way sign signalling a fork in the road, a track heads east through the woodland. Although not signposted as such, this is the **Pingo Trail**, so follow it. Walk through woodland to reach a gate that opens onto a scrubby area. Turn right here, following a short boardwalk. The Pingo Trail slides through a hedge to reach an open area dotted with pingos; the air above one particularly impressive example whooshes with dragonflies. When you are done admiring the wildlife, follow signposts through the wood, past another gate, and across two bridges until you arrive at the car park.

What to look out for –

Songline sculpture

The standing stone just south of Thompson Water is one of Tom Perkins' sculptures which form the Norfolk Songline. This multimedia project honours the Peddars Way. A poem inscribed onto the stone commemorates both our ancestors and ancient footpaths.

10 *Thornham and Holme Dunes*

7 miles / 11.2 km

On the longest walk in the book, you explore saltmarsh and estuary, sand dunes and grazing marshes, tranquil villages and chalky fields. Partly following the Peddars Way and the Norfolk Coastal Path, the route takes in the National Nature Reserve at Holme Dunes, a renowned location for students of bird migration and a breeding site for the rare natterjack toad. Make time for a picnic on Thornham beach, where you can combine beach cricket with spotting rare (and excitingly named) insects such as dune tiger-beetle and bee-wolf!

The Walk

1 Arriving at the car park, admire fishing boats moored by the jetty and scan the saltmarsh eastwards for marsh harrier and shorebirds such as redshank. Then walk west, crossing the sluice gate, to reach the **Peddars Way and Norfolk Coast Path**. This hard-surfaced path runs north then west along a raised embankment. Below you, saltmarsh lies to your right (north) and fields to your left.

2 After ¾ mile (1.2 km), you come alongside **Broad Water**, a long lake

Terrain Hard path, boardwalk, sandy sections, country lanes and farm tracks.

Map OS Explorer 250 Norfolk Coast West.

Starting point Staithe Lane car park, Thornham (GR TF 728442).

How to get there & parking Leave the A149 coast road at the western edge of Thornham village, ⅓ mile (0.5 km) east of the Drove Orchards shopping and food complex, heading north along Staithe Lane. Use the car park at the road end, just after an isolated barn on the right (east). **Sat Nav:** PE36 6LT.

Refreshments The Norfolk Wildlife Trust operates a café at its Holme Dunes reserve, during reserve opening hours Mar–Oct: 10-16h30; ☎ 01485 525240. In Thornham, The Orange Tree ⊕ theorangetreethornham.co.uk is an award-winning gastropub with rooms and, at Drove Orchards, Eric's is a stellar fish 'n' chips restaurant ⊕ ericsfishandchips.com.

stretching to the west. Now flanked by sand dunes, the path becomes a boardwalk to protect that fragile habitat. Should you fancy diverting to the beach, follow any of the narrow tracks leading north through the dunes. If not, continue along the boardwalk as it runs past the entrance to the **Norfolk Ornithologists' Association reserve** and through the pine belt. At the end of the trees, there is a crossroads where you can access the beach to the right (north) or nip left (south) to the **Norfolk Wildlife Trust visitor centre and café.**

③ The boardwalk emerges from the pines and enters the main part of the Wildlife Trust reserve – an area of sand dunes with extensive patches of scrub, with the odd concrete World War II defence dotted around. Should you wish to venture off the **Peddars Way** to explore the reserve, you must buy a permit from the visitor centre (no permit is needed to walk the public footpath). Migrant birds may skulk in clumps of elder, bramble and sea buckthorn; the latter's orange berries can be pressed into a rather tart juice. Grassy areas are grazed by Konik ponies. Hidden among the reserve dunes are a few shallow ponds, which provide breeding sites for the rare natterjack toad. The path passes tidal inlets favoured by curlew and oystercatcher (with **Gore Point** beyond) then rubs shoulders with the

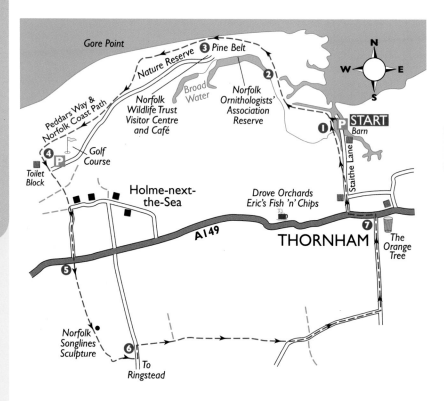

reserve entrance road by a small parking lot. Continue along the footpath for 1¼ miles (1.9 km), past several impressive-looking houses, until you reach a golf course.

④ At a major junction of paths, the **Peddars Way** turns left (south) along the broad, sandy track towards **Holme-next-the-Sea**. By a toilet block and car park, the **Peddars Way** follows a leafy country lane, along which you continue south for ¾ mile (1.2 km), skirting **Holme** village.

⑤ Cross the A149 and seek out the **Peddars Way** opposite, access to which is slightly hidden behind a bus stop. The footpath rises gradually and weaves between two sunny, sheltered hedgerows. Where the hedgerows cease, you come to a lichen-encrusted standing stone. This is one of five sculptures in the Norfolk Songlines project (see also Thompson Common, page 47).

⑥ The **Peddars Way** joins a country lane just north of **Ringstead** village, opposite a large, modern house with a huge garden. Turn left here, and

continue for 100 yards until you see a chalky farm track off to the right (east), signposted **Ringstead Circular Walk**. Take this track, which runs through fields and offers sea views down to your left (north). After 1 mile (1.5 km), it joins a hedge-flanked country lane. Follow this east, ignoring both a public footpath to your right (south) and a narrow road to your left (north). After ½ mile (0.8 km), you reach a T junction. Turn left here and continue downhill along the quiet road for ²/₃ mile (1 km) until you reach the A149 at **Thornham** village.

⑦ Turn left (west) along the main road, following the pavement for 300 yards until you reach **Staithe Lane** to your right (north). Turn north along the Lane and bear left at the fork. Soon you will see the isolated barn and saltmarsh that herald your return to the car park. For your final 300 yards, you can choose between sticking to the road or climbing onto the embankment to your left (west), which runs alongside a creek.

What to look out for –

Sea buckthorn

A classic bush of coastal Norfolk, notably on sand dunes, is sea buckthorn. The grey-green colour of the rosemary-like sprigs makes this plant easy to identify. In late summer, spotting one is made even more straightforward by the bright orange berries that adorn this sun-loving plant. Many people harvest the berries, which are vitamin powerpacks.

11 Overstrand and Cromer

3¾ miles / 6 km

Although Norfolk is renowned for its flatness, we do have a few places where contours trouble the map. One such area is the north-east coast between Overstrand and Cromer, where cliffs of soft clay reach a heady 75 yards in height. This walk, out along the beach and back along the escarpment, enables you to admire the cliffs (while they still exist) and to use the height to look far out to sea.

The route also takes in the best bits of Cromer, a Victorian seaside town that is enjoying rebirth as a foodie Mecca thanks to the clustering of fine independent eateries. Cromer is also renowned for its pier (particularly if you enjoy traditional seaside entertainment).

The Walk

1 From the clifftop car park, follow the sign for **Paston Way** east. Just after an open area with benches, a steep concrete path drops left (north) to the beach. Unless you want a cuppa at the **Cliff Top Café** (which lies just to your right) first, descend the path to reach the beach.

2 At the foot of the cliffs, turn left and walk for about 2 miles (3.2 km) west-north-west along the beach to **Cromer**. This follows the **National Trail**. For the first few hundred yards, a wooden groyne runs parallel to the

The Facts

Terrain Beach, pavement or paved path, and undulating footpath.

Map OS Explorer 252 Norfolk Coast East.

Starting point Pauls Lane car park, Pauls Lane, Overstrand (GR TG 247410).

How to get there & parking Entering Cromer from the south along the A140, turn right onto Cromwell Road. Head straight over at the double roundabout, following signs to Overstrand. Continue broadly south-east, past the Royal Cromer Golf Club on your left (north). When you reach Overstrand, turn first left (north) into Pauls Lane, and follow this to the car park at the cliff top. **Sat Nav:** NR27 0PF.

Refreshments In Overstrand, Cliff Top Café is just 100 yards from the car park, on Cliff Road. It serves breakfasts and simple lunches ⊕ clifftopholidays.co.uk/cliff-top-cafe-norfolk. On the main road in Overstrand, the Potting Shed café is excellent ⊕ gardencentreoverstrand.co.uk/tearoom-cafe-overstrand-cromer. In Cromer, arguably the best fish 'n' chips is served by Number 1 Cromer on New Street, which is run by local celebrity chef Galton Blackiston ⊕ no1cromer.com. Alternatively try the Rocket House Café above the RNLI Henry Blogg museum ⊕ rockethousecafe.co.uk.

cliff, before seeming to abandon hope below some of the steepest cliffs and stuttering to an end. Other groynes stride into the sea, perpendicular to the cliffs. The slumping cliffs become increasingly vegetated as you approach Cromer, with sycamores and sea buckthorn among the plants helping stabilise the slope. Ahead of you is Cromer pier.

3 As you reach a line of beach huts, you leave the sandy ground to join a paved walkway. Continue along this, past the beach huts, until you reach the first fishing boats, which mark the start of the esplanade proper. Between here and Cromer pier is the **RNLI museum** (which houses the **Rocket House Café**) and various cafés and watersports establishments.

4 Feel free to stroll along the pier, which was built in 1900 to replace one destroyed in storms five years earlier. You could even go crabbing! Then walk up the zigzag path at the base of the pier to reach the town centre. At the top, a sign indicates that you are at the start of the **Weavers'**

autumn

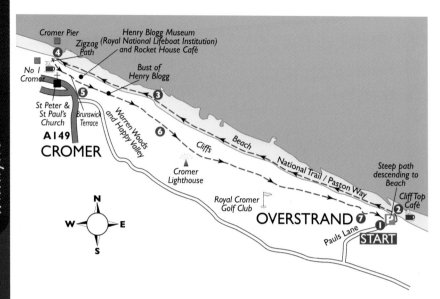

Way, a long-distance footpath that features in another walk in this book (page 21). Turn left past **Hotel de Paris** then bear right onto **Jetty Street**, which features terraced houses of different colours. At **St Peter and Paul's Church**, turn left along **East Cliff**, past a taxi rank. Beyond the **Red Lion** restaurant, take **Brunswick Terrace** (a narrow path with railings on either side) which curves to the right, overlooking the RNLI museum.

❺ Cross the cobbled gangway and continue straight, following the footpath east as it weaves past a cottage and small park. On your right is a memorial bust in honour of lifeboatman **Henry Blogg**. The paved path rises gently until the **National Trail** (marked with acorn signs) is signposted left down to the beach; ignore this and continue straight along the clifftop, with its commanding views. Head past a seating area with benches and coastguard lookout, subsequently passing (or exploring, as you fancy) **Warren Woods** and **Happy Valley**.

❻ Ignore public footpaths off to your right (south) and continue along the head of the cliffs. The path undulates considerably as it weaves through gorse and bramble. **Cromer Lighthouse**, set back to your right (south), signals the start of the **Royal Cromer Golf Club**, which you follow for all bar the final few hundred yards of the walk. Ensure that you tread a fine line by staying on the public footpath for the full 1¼ miles (2 km), neither venturing too close to the crumbling edge nor onto the golf course.

7 The path passes some houses on the right, which mark the start of **Overstrand**. After a rectangular green area, you duck through a belt of trees to emerge in the car park, a flagpole and playground to your right.

What to look out for –

Henry Blogg

The Royal National Lifeboat Institution museum is dedicated to **Henry Blogg**, Cromer lifeboatman, hero and (with the assistance of his crew) saviour of 873 lives across 387 rescue missions. Blogg served for 53 years, during which time the RNLI awarded him seven medals (more than any other lifeboatman), and he also received the George Cross and the British Empire Medal.

12 Cley and Salthouse

4¾ miles / 7.6 km

Perhaps no part of Norfolk better symbolises the tug of war between Man and Nature than the stretch of coast between the postcard-perfect village of Cley next the Sea and neighbouring Salthouse. Twice in recent years a raging North Sea has invaded the land, enabling seals to swim along the A149, the main road that lies the best part of a mile from the normal shoreline.

This walk treads over shingle, traverses reedbeds, pauses at lagoons amidst rough grassland and rambles through damp woodland. There should be plenty of fauna and flora to see along the route. Brent and pink-footed geese graze in the fields. Sea aster and yellow horned poppy may flower even as late as October – the former along the shingle, the latter by the saltmarsh. In the reedbeds of Cley Marshes reserve bearded tits can be prominent in autumn as family parties bounce around excitedly. The willow-rich scrub at Walsey Hills is often a favoured haunt of birdwatchers on the lookout for a Siberian warbler or two.

The Facts

Terrain Hard-surface permissive paths, often muddy or boggy public footpaths, and shingle (hard walking!).

Map OS Explorer 251 Norfolk Coast Central.

Starting point The Norfolk Wildlife Trust car park by Cley Marshes reserve visitor centre, Coast Road, east of Cley next the Sea village (GR TG 054440).

How to get there & parking Take the A149 east from Cley next the Sea village (known locally simply as 'Cley'). The visitor centre and car park are visible (and signposted) 300 yards beyond Old Woman's Lane. **Sat Nav:** NR25 7SA.

Refreshments The café at Cley Marshes visitor centre offers light lunches, cakes and drinks. The Dun Cow is an excellent pub just 400 yards off route, in Salthouse village.
⊕ salthouseduncow.com.

The Walk

❶ From the car park by the spectacular **Norfolk Wildlife Trust visitor centre**, cross the A149. Here a reserve trail runs parallel to the main road on its northern side. Follow the path left (west) towards **Cley** village as it fringes a reedbed-lined channel where you might spot water vole and late dragonflies. After ¼ mile (400 yards), an opportunity exists to turn right (north) to reach three hides which offer purviews over lagoons that are often crammed with ducks and waders. (To access the hides, you must buy a permit from the visitor centre if you are not a Norfolk Wildlife Trust member.) Otherwise continue straight on until you reach **Beach Road**, which heads north to the sea.

❷ Turn right (north) here, and take the first opportunity to leave the road and climb the embankment on its western side. This slightly elevated position gives you a vista over the reserve to the right (east) and saltmarsh to your left (west). Continue along the embankment until you reach the **North Sea** at **Beach Road car park**.

❸ Head right (east) across the car park, passing a brick shelter with seats that hardy birdwatchers use to watch seabirds passing offshore. You are now walking over shingle along the **Norfolk Coast Path**. You

autumn

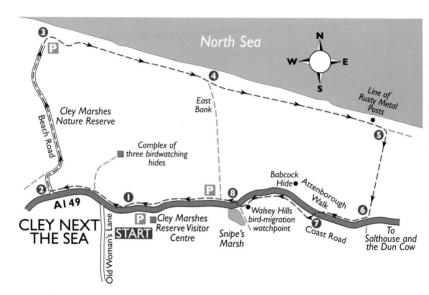

may find this hard going – two steps forward, one step back… To your left (north) is the sea; watch out for seals and gannets. To your right, a rough field, often occupied by brent geese, gives way to the remains of a birdwatching hide (destroyed in storms) which looks out over a 'scrape' (a shallow lagoon).

4 Just over ¾ mile (1.3 km) from **Beach Road car park**, just after a saline lagoon, a public footpath strides towards you from the south. This is **East Bank**, which used to serve as a hallowed meeting place for birdwatchers from the 1950s onwards. A rather Modernist-looking hide stands a few hundred yards south of the junction; feel free to divert and look for some birdlife. Alternatively, continue straight on (east) along the coast path. A tall shingle bank rises to your left (north), with a lower, grassier ridge to your right (south) that conceals your presence from birdlife on the saline lagoon beyond. At the end of the pool, both banks disappear, leaving you to walk on open shingle alongside a fence. After ½ mile, a line of rusty, wrought-iron posts emerges from the shingle.

5 As these start to disappear, the fence bends inland to the right (south). Follow this to reach a broad public footpath that stands proud between two ditches. Continue south-south-west along this, passing muddy pools and a complex of gates until you reach a tiny informal car park by the A149.

6 Turn right just before the main road through a gate that announces

your arrival at the Norfolk Wildlife Trust's '**Attenborough Walk**', named in honour of broadcaster, naturalist and national icon Sir David. After 400 yards, you reach another set of gates. To your right lies **Babcock Hide**, which you may wish to visit should you have both the inclination and a permit (which you can get from the Wildlife Trust Visitor Centre).

7 Otherwise, turn left across a brick bridge and cross the A149 to its south side. Turn right (west) along a public footpath, which soon heads slightly uphill towards some pine trees. At the crest of the hill, look right (north) for a splendid view over **Salthouse marshes**. Then follow the public footpath south as it borders scrub that forms the southern part of the bird-migration watchpoint of **Walsey Hills**. At the junction of footpaths turn sharp right to walk north-north-west. Continue for 200 yards through willow-dominated scrub to reach the A149 by a pool called **Snipe's Marsh**. A small layby lies to your right.

8 Cross back over the road, and walk carefully left (west) along the verge until you reach a car park at the southern end of **East Bank**. Here you rejoin the visitor trail along the southern edge of **Cley Marshes reserve**. Continue along the path for ½ mile (0.8 km) to reach the visitor centre car park.

What to look out for –

Cley Marshes visitor centre

This walk would be incomplete without entering **Cley Marshes visitor centre**. The ground-hugging building is visually stunning, exhibiting a distinctive double-curved, sedum-moss-covered roof and enormous plate-glass windows. The views over the reserve are magnificent, and a visit is enhanced by regular exhibitions (including in the Simon Aspinall environmental education centre immediately to the left of the photo), interactive displays, a decent café and a well-stocked shop. Best of all is the range of sustainable features and materials that minimise the environmental impact of the building on its surroundings. A design *and* environmental success.

13 Holkham and Burnham Overy Dunes

5²/₃ miles / 9 km

Gwyneth Paltrow strode across its salted-caramel vastness at the close of the film *Shakespeare in Love*. Leading travel writers recently voted its unspoilt magnificence the best beach in Britain. Topped by Norfolk's famed big blue skies, Holkham Beach is genuinely jaw-dropping. Yet the expansive, liberating strand is just one highlight of this walk through a National Nature Reserve that encompasses grazing marshes thronged with wild geese, clandestine woodland dominated by a triumvirate of towering pines, swirling dune-heath harbouring natterjack toads, and muddy saltmarsh soothing tidal ravages.

The Walk _____

1 Before you start, scan grazing marshes to the west for flocks of pink-footed geese, wigeon and teal. Then walk to the north end of the line of cars, beyond the gate. At the junction, rather than go straight on (north) to the bay of **Holkham Gap** or right (east) towards **Wells Woods**, turn left (west) along a broad track that saunters through the attractive woodland

Terrain A combination of hard-surface tracks and sandy paths; both are usually dry.

Map OS Explorer 251 Norfolk Coast Central.

Starting point Pay-and-display car park at Holkham Gap, at the north end of Lady Anne's Drive, Holkham (GR TF 890447).

How to get there & parking Holkham village lies on the A149 coast road, 1½ miles (2.5 km) west of Wells-next-the-Sea. As you reach Holkham, turn north at the crossroads by The Victoria Inn. This leads along Lady Anne's Drive to the car park. **Sat Nav:** NR23 1RJ.

Refreshments There are good options at either end of Lady Anne's Drive. At the northern tip, by the car park, is The Lookout café that opened in 2018 ⊕ holkham.co.uk/stay-eat/the-lookout. To the south is The Victoria Inn, a top-notch gastropub with rooms ⊕ holkham.co.uk/stay-eat/the-victoria-inn.

of **Holkham Pines**. After 600 yards, you pass a stinky pond that, despite its obviously sulphuric nature, somehow attracts little grebes.

2 Three hundred yards on, you reach a boardwalk that heads north, passing by a bird hide en route to the beach. The **George Washington hide** offers fine views over the grazing marsh, so is worth a stop. This is also a particularly good place to spot migrant songbirds – regular jewels include yellow-browed warbler. Then continue west along the track, admiring the location and garden of **Meals House**.

3 After another 500 yards, in a belt of pines, you reach the 'cross-tracks'. To the north are the dunes at **Burrow Gap**. To the south is a tower hide (**Joe Jordan hide**) that offers an elevated purview over the freshmarsh. Indulge yourself by deviating in either direction, then return to the main drag, continuing straight on (west) through increasingly scrubby woodland.

4 After ½ mile (0.8 km), when you see a five-bar gate ahead, the path dog-legs right (north) then immediately left (west). You quickly emerge from scattered pines into **Burnham Overy Dunes**. The terrain becomes sandy, with bramble-dominated scrub to your right (north). The path heads along the fence line; continue through the dune-heath for ⅔ mile (1.2 km) until you reach a scrubby patch with a large apple tree.

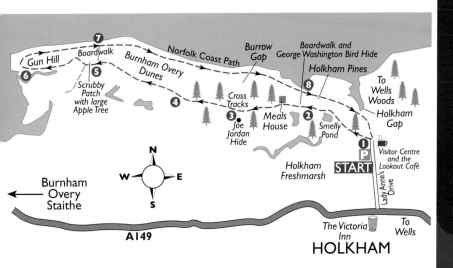

autumn

5 Here the path jinks through the brambles to join a short boardwalk. Follow this right (north) for 50 yards, then leave it to the left (west). Ahead, ½ mile (0.8 km) to the west, is the raised dune that marks **Gun Hill**. Head towards this, following the small path that snakes between the dense, low-lying vegetation by the saltmarsh and the dunes.

6 Keep **Gun Hill** to your right and the saltmarsh to your left. Admire a small wooden houseboat and the ruins of a building adjacent to a stunted sycamore tree – the only one of its kind out here. Continue to the dune

ridge, where you can look west at **Scolt Head island**, which lies across a channel. (Don't be tempted to wade across!) Then double-back on yourself (east), this time keeping **Gun Hill** to your right. Continue east through the dunes, following either your whim or one of the indistinct paths, until you reach the northern end of the boardwalk along which you walked briefly in step 5. Make for the signpost, which signals the **Norfolk Coast Path**.

7 Follow this public footpath east. It ploughs through the dunes before jinking left (north-east) then right (east) to run along the south side of the beach, with the dunes to your right. After ½ mile (0.8 km), the western edge of **Holkham Pines** will emerge to your right, beyond the dunes. By now the enormity of **Holkham Beach** will be apparent. Feel free to explore it, to stay along the **Norfolk Coast Path** or to take a parallel path along the north side of the pines.

8 About a mile (1.6 km) after you first draw level with the pines, look for a raised wooden viewing point to your right, at the fringe of the forest. Make for this (which is the north end of the boardwalk that you passed in step 2), then turn left (east) and walk along the northern side of the pines all the way to **Holkham Gap**. Make for the innermost point of this triangular 'bay', and follow the boardwalk past a fenced-off triangle back to **Lady Anne's Drive**.

What to look out for –

Pines

At some point during the walk, take time out to wander in the pinewoods. The silence may come as a surprise; needles cushion noisy footfall and the tall canopy acts as a windbreak. Try to differentiate between the three types of pines growing here. Corsican pine has a grey trunk and small cones; the trunk of Scots pine turns orange as it rises; and Maritime pine has large cones in tree-top clusters. All were planted in the late 19th century.

14 **Brancaster**

4¼ miles / 6.8 km

The remnants of a **Roman fort**, an expansive bay beloved of kitesurfers, the breeziest of royal golf courses, a flint-rich village and Norfolk's wildest saltmarshes make for a perfect autumn walk. While there is no longer anything to see of the Roman outpost of Branodunum, that is no excuse for not imagining the vivacity of its past. Brancaster is north-west Norfolk at its best.

The Walk _____

❶ Exit the car park onto **Broad Lane**, with the **Royal West Norfolk Golf Club** building to your right (north). Tempting though it may be to immediately venture onto the wide sands at **Brancaster Bay**, save that treat for the end of the walk. Instead, turn left (south) to head inland. Climb the short bank behind the toilet block and take the raised public footpath south. To your right (west) are rough fields and reedbeds. To your left (east), across the road, is saltmarsh from where the cries of curlew and brent geese may emanate. Continue along the embankment, descending by a concrete structure to pass a huge willow tree.

❷ As you reach some houses, two public footpaths meet at a T junction. Turn left (east) to reach **Broad Lane**. Turn left (north) then immediately right (east) to follow the **National Trail** sign along the public footpath.

NORFOLK *Year Round Walks*

Terrain A mixture of hard paths, occasionally muddy tracks, boardwalk, grassy field, beach, quiet village road and pavement.

Map OS Explorer 250 Norfolk Coast West.

Starting point Brancaster beach car park (pay and display), Broad Lane, Brancaster (GR TF 771450).

How to get there & parking Take the A149 north then east from Hunstanton until you reach Brancaster. Upon entering the village from the west, take the first left (north) along Broad Lane, almost opposite the poorly signposted B1153 turn. Follow signs to the car park, which lies at the northernmost end of the road, opposite Royal West Norfolk Golf Club. **Sat Nav:** PE31 8AX.

Refreshments Two pubs within 300 yards of the route offer excellent dining, decent ales and boutique accommodation: Ship Hotel in Brancaster ⊕ shiphotelnorfolk.co.uk and Titchwell Manor ⊕ titchwellmanor.com.

Continue for about ⅔ mile (1 km), mainly along a narrow boardwalk, admiring several large gardens that greet the footpath from the right (south).

3 At the end of a belt of trees, you will see a gate to your right (south). Go through this and pause at an information board to read about the

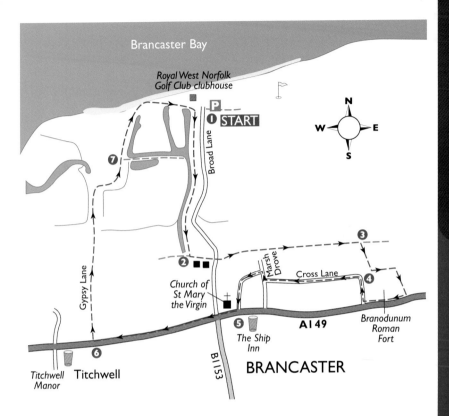

Roman fort of Branodunum. At this point you are standing pretty much at the landing beach for Roman naval and trading vessels. Two paths now lead through a grassy field. Take the right one to head roughly south. After 100 yards, take the central path of three, which leads through a kissing gate onto a vehicular track. Continue straight across to pass through another kissing gate, marked with a National Trust sign. This roughly square field is the location of the fort, which featured in the Channel 4 TV series *Time Team* during 2013. Nothing is visible but grass, so explore via your imagination as you stroll clockwise around the field. Return through the kissing gate onto the vehicular track.

❹ Turn left here, cross a cattle grid and join **Cross Lane** which you follow right as it heads north then west. Follow this quiet road for 600 yards through the edge of the village. At a T junction, turn right (north) onto **Marsh Drove**. After 50 yards, take the public footpath through the barriers to your left (west). This brings you to **London Street**, where you turn left (south) to reach the A149 and village centre.

autumn

5 Turn right (west) here, and walk along the pavement along the north side of the main road. Pass the **Church of St Mary the Virgin**, cross **Broad Lane**, pass **Manor Farm** and keep walking west along the pavement.

6 Half-a-mile (¾ km) after Broad Lane, you reach a pull-in on the right (north), which has space for a few cars. Here a public footpath runs north along **Gypsy Lane**, weaving through a narrow belt of woodland that mixes hawthorn scrub with oak trees and ivy bushes. On sunny days this stretch can be alive with ivy bees, hoverflies and dragonflies. Continue north, emerging from the woodland just after a display board that confesses that you are actually in **RSPB Titchwell reserve**. A hard-surface path now heads straight between reedbeds, then runs past saltmarsh on your left (west; can you spot the World War II lookout posts?) and grazing marsh to your right (east). Follow the embankment as it turns 90° right, ignoring the suggestion on the OS map to head straight on along a public footpath (which would involve crossing a deep and muddy creek then wading through dense suaeda vegetation).

7 Follow the public footpath until it reaches the golf clubhouse (ignoring the path that heads due east). Here, rather than heading straight back to the car, take the opportunity to scamper north onto the beach at **Brancaster Bay**. The strand here is expansive – in Norfolk, second only to Holkham Bay (page 61) in its vastness and family-friendliness. Wander as far as you fancy here, in either direction, before returning to your car.

What to look out for –

Kitesurfers

Visit Brancaster Bay on a breezy day and you will not fail to notice kitesurfers skim across the waves before flying through the air. Although the history of kitesurfing can be traced back to 1903, the sport proper was born in the Netherlands in 1977.

15 Horsey

3½ miles / 5.6 km

The star of this walk amidst sand dunes, through grazing marshes and beneath a sentinel windmill is unequivocal. We are within a common crane's bugle of one of Norfolk's most famous broads. The colony of grey seals in the dunes at Horsey has rapidly become one of the country's biggest, with more than 1,500 pups born each year. In 2017, an astonishing 1,818 chubby cuties greeted the world. How many will you count on your visit?

The common cranes – the birds rather than the machines – are harder to spot than the seals. A population of 60-odd individuals has made the vicinity their home for several decades, but they tend to lope amidst the highest vegetation around, making them tricky to see. No such problems of visibility when they take to the air, however. With long wings flapped majestically and neck and legs extended, their elegance is unparalleled. Seeing one (or, better, a flock) calls for a celebration. Just as well that one of Norfolk's cosiest and foodiest pubs is just yards from the route…

The Walk _____

❶ Surrounded by trees and bushes, **Horsey Mill car park** is surprisingly attractive. A bog garden takes pride of place in a freshly designed flower-

autumn

The Facts

Terrain Footpaths, permissive paths and a roadside verge, encompassing grazing pasture (which can get boggy), sand dunes and firm tracks. After rain, rubber boots are advisable.

Map OS Explorer OL40 The Broads.

Starting point Horsey Mill National Trust car park (members free; otherwise pay and display), Marsh Road, Horsey (GR TG 457223).

How to get there & parking Leave the A149 at Martham, heading east into that village, following signs for West Somerton. Turn left at the Y junction by The Lion pub. Continue north for 1¾ miles (2.8 km) until you see the sign for Horsey Mill car park on the left (west). **Sat Nav: NR29 4EE.**

Refreshments One of my favourite Norfolk pubs, Nelson Head ⊕ thenelsonhead.com is barely 50 yards off the route, so makes a perfect stop. Cosy, decent beer and fine fayre – the perfect triumvirate. The 1940s-themed café at Poppylands (☎ 01493 393393) is barely any further from the main drag either! Finally, the National Trust runs a small café at Horsey Mill car park (open daily 10–16h30).

rich area, and a footpath leads west to a jetty on **Horsey Mere** from which boat trips leave regularly in search of wildlife. It is also just 90 yards from **Horsey Windpump** itself, which marks the first point of interest on your walk. Head to the road and walk a few yards south, past the **National Trust café**, to admire the windpump. Then cross the road carefully and cross a short bridge to follow a permissive path east across rough grassland (for now, ignore the path to your left/north, although you will come back along it). Distant wind turbines lie to your right and the tall sand dunes at the coast are visible 1⅓ miles (2 km) ahead of you. Beyond a copse, the path turns left through a gate, becomes a stony track and heads roughly north, with damp, tussocky grassland to your right (east) and a reed-lined channel to your left (west).

② Passing through another gate, you reach a narrow country lane. Fifty yards to your left (west) is the **Nelson Head** pub, but you turn right (east). After 50 yards, take the left fork by a cottage. Birdwatchers call this the Nelson Head track, and it leads north-east all the way to the sand dunes.

autumn

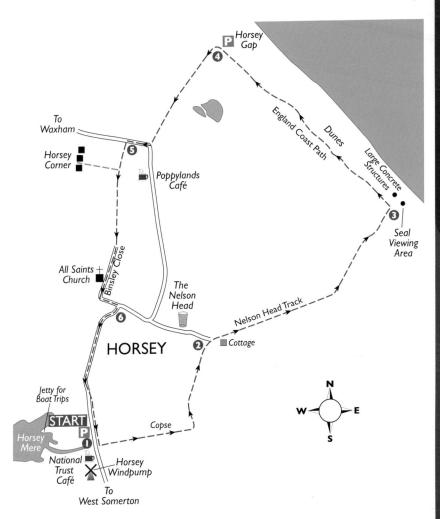

3 Your arrival at the dunes in autumn or early winter should be greeted by plenty of information about the grey seal breeding season. To see the seals, follow signs to the viewing area slightly to your right (south-east), which is wardened by volunteers to minimise disturbance to these sensitive mammals. Once you had gawped (and counted!), return to the **England Coast Path** at the base of the dunes and walk just under a mile (1.5 km) north-west to **Horsey Gap**. Keep the dunes to your right (and stick to the path to avoid erosion) and keep an eye on the rough grazing pasture to your left for short-eared owl and harriers. Occasional bushes

may attract migrant birds, and stonechats may hop ahead of you along the fenceline.

4 Shortly after you pass a World War II sea defence atop a dune on the right (north), you reach a markedly scrubby area. Pass through a gate to reach the expansive **Horsey Gap car park**. If you are a birdwatcher, you might want to check the bushes for passage migrants. If not, simply head for the exit and follow the broad track (south-west) through dense willow scrub and open grassland back to the 'main road'. **Poppylands Café** now lies just to your left (south).

5 Jink right (west) long the road for 50 yards, before turning left (south) onto a public footpath that runs between fields and eventually alongside a hedge. Ignore the path off to your right (west, leading past houses at **Horsey Corner** to **Brograve Mill**). The footpath joins a country lane (**Binsley Close**) as it reaches several cottages – some with a thatched roof. At **All Saints Church** (which also has a thatched roof), the road and path turn sharp left (east-south-east). Follow this, with a small football field to your left, and take the first right (south) to rejoin the 'main' road by some cottages.

❻ Cross the road and walk along a narrow footpath on its eastern verge. At the second thatched cottage, a sign on your left directs you along a permissive path behind a hedge. **Horsey Windpump** is now visible ahead. The path takes you to the small bridge that you crossed in step 1, which signals your return to **Horsey Mill car park**.

What to look out for –

Grey seal

There are two species of seal in Britain: grey and common (or harbour). Our country hosts roughly half the world's grey seals. It is this species that has colonised the dunes at Horsey in recent years ⊕ friendsofhorseyseals.co.uk. Although we think of seals as marine animals, they must come ashore to breed. Technically, then, a male (or bull) grey seal is Britain's heaviest land mammal. The colony is called a rookery and, at Horsey, is usually occupied from October until January. If you visit the Horsey colony, please respect the animals, staying at least ten yards away.

16 *Caistor St Edmund*

3½ miles / 5.7 km

Just 2 miles (3 km) south of Norwich, this route investigates an old Roman town ('Venta Icenorum') and honours the rebel queen who tackled the might of the occupying Empire. The southern segment of the walk follows the Boudicca Way, named after the eponymous British Celtic Iceni warrior (also known as Boadicea) who led an uprising against the occupying Roman forces in AD60/61.

The walk also traverses the fields of High Ash Farm, where permissive paths grant public access to land that, inspiringly, is managed specifically with wildlife in mind.

The Walk

1 The first part of the walk (steps 1–2) is a loop enabling you to explore the **Venta Icenorum** (Caistor Roman Town). Head through the kissing gate at the north end of the car park. Take the rough path leading to a steep bank, which marks the south-eastern tip of the roughly square Roman feature. Ascend the bank (which forms the town ramparts) and admire the flint tower of **Caistor St Edmund Church**. The church was apparently built on the line of a Roman street; there is evidence of Christianity here from at least the 10th century.

2 Head left (west) along the embankment, so that you circumnavigate

Terrain Grassy and muddy paths (rubber boots recommended), and two country lanes. Flat with the odd slight incline.

Map OS Explorer 237 Norwich.

Starting point Free car park for the Roman town, along Stoke Road, immediately south-west of Caistor St Edmund hamlet (GR TG 232032).

How to get there & parking From the A47/A140 underpass south of Norwich, take the minor road leading east to Caistor St Edmund. Reaching the village after a mile (1.5 km), turn right (south) at the crossroads and use the car park on the right (west) after ½ mile (0.8 km). **Sat Nav:** NR14 8QL.

Refreshments In Stoke Holy Cross, 1 mile (1.5 km) south, The Wildebeest is a fine gastropub ⊕ thewildebeest.co.uk and Stoke Mill a smart restaurant, open for lunch and dinner ⊕ stokemill.co.uk.

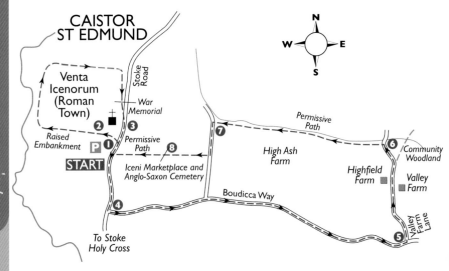

CAISTOR ST EDMUND

Venta Icenorum (Roman Town)

Raised Embankment

Stoke Road

War Memorial

START

Permissive Path

Iceni Marketplace and Anglo-Saxon Cemetery

To Stoke Holy Cross

High Ash Farm

Boudicca Way

Permissive Path

Highfield Farm

Community Woodland

Valley Farm

Valley Farm Lane

winter

the Venta anticlockwise, along a marked trail. The Roman town may not look much nowadays – a raised grassy embankment, with occasional fragments of wall. So pause at the interpretative signs to learn about what you are seeing and imagine how Roman life here unfolded in a community that was actually not much smaller than Roman Colchester. On the final stretch of the circuit, when you are heading south, you come to a war memorial that commemorates parishioners who succumbed during World War I. Here a path leads left (east) down to the road. Take this to join the road, which is where you join the **Boudicca Way**.

3 Walk south along the road/**Boudicca Way**, with fields and a rookery to your left (east) and the car park to your right (west). Walk along the verge wherever possible, keeping a keen eye out for cars.

4 After ⅔ mile (1 km), just after some cottages, turn left at the first road junction, continuing along the **Boudicca Way**. This is a quieter lane, with a slight upwards incline in its early stages. As you approach a junction with a road coming in from your left (north), finches such as linnet and chaffinch should start to appear in the weedy fields and hedgerows of **High Ash Farm**. Look carefully among them and you may spot the flashing white rumps of brambling, a winter speciality in these parts. After a further ¾ mile (1.2 km), you pass some houses then turn left (north) along **Valley Farm Lane**.

5 This lane twists as it descends, passing **Valley Farm** and **Highfield Farm**. Allow **Boudicca Way** to head off to the right (north-east, towards Norwich), instead continuing along the lane for 100 yards until you reach an incipient, triangular community woodland on the right (east), flanking a brook.

6 Turn left (west) here, through a five-bar gate marked with the words 'High Ash Farm'. Walk roughly west along this permissive path for ¾ mile (1.2 km). Fields lie on both sides: watch out for yellowhammers in the hedges and skylarks overhead. After an oval-shaped pond on the left, you briefly enter a deciduous woodland before arriving at a narrow road.

7 Turn left (south) here, heading uphill for just under 200 yards, before you follow another permissive path right (west).

8 A further 200 yards along this path, a group of pine trees announces a point of interest – a 'county monument', no less. This transpires to be an Anglo-Saxon cemetery and Iceni marketplace. Burial urns excavated here are now showcased in Norwich Museum. A sign advises that the burial plot was located on high ground 'to shorten the spirits' journey to the heavens'. Continue west along the path to the road, where you now find yourself opposite the car park where you started.

winter

What to look out for –

Winter finches

In winter, finches throng to High Ash Farm's weedy fields. The most common is linnet, which is small with white flashes in its wing and tail. Chaffinch is also common; both sexes have bold white bands in the wing, and the male is largely pink. Best of all is brambling, which is easily identified in flight due to its discrete white rump. The male (right) has lovely burnt-orange feathering on its underparts and shoulder.

17 Snettisham

4½ miles / 7.2 km

Snettisham is uncompromising. The land stares west into the vastness of The Wash, one of Britain's finest estuaries – a realm that is alternately unrelenting tidal mudflat or unending sea. The sky stretches impossibly wide as well as towering all-mightily high – and the wind, if there is one, knows no bounds. Leaving behind the bleakness of stubborn dwellings fronting the coast, this walk strides along the estuary shoreline before weaving through the lagoons and saltmarsh of one of the RSPB's most renowned nature reserves. Marvel at the immense flocks of pink-footed geese, or at gargantuan, billowing clouds of shorebirds escaping the rising tide. Whether or not you are a confirmed birdwatcher, either spectacle will exhilarate. Make no mistake, everything about this wintry walk is both wild and big.

The Walk _____

1 From **Beach Road car park**, head south along footpath 35, which follows the top of the shingle beach, the caravan site to its left (east). To your right (west), **The Wash** estuary opens out; on a fine day, you might be able to see across its entirety, all the way to Lincolnshire.

2 Walking south along a concrete path, you pass further chalets and cabins, some ramshackle and others lovingly preserved. The present-day occupants have a royal heritage. In 1908, Queen Alexandra (wife of

The Facts

Terrain A mixture of sandy paths along and near the beach, shingle tracks, tarmac road and narrow muddy paths. Stout footwear – perhaps rubber boots – recommended (thick socks too if it is cold!).

Map OS Explorer 250 Norfolk Coast West.

Starting point Snettisham beach car park, sited where Beach Road ends at The Wash, west of Snettisham village (GR TF 648335).

How to get there & parking From the A149, 2¾ miles (4.4 km) south of Heacham and just south-west of Snettisham village, turn west along Beach Road, following signs to the RSPB reserve. Continue for 2 miles (3.2 km) to the very end of the road, ignoring the sign to the left (south) for the RSPB car park and passing beyond the caravan site. Use the beach car park (pay and display). **Sat Nav:** PE31 7RA.

Refreshments In Snettisham village, the Rose and Crown is an award-winning village inn, with low ceilings, twisting passages and fine food ⊕ roseandcrownsnettisham.co.uk. In the same village is another award-winner, The Old Bank Bistro, which prides itself on being 'home away from home' ⊕ theoldbankbistro.co.uk; open Thu–Sat for lunch and dinner, and Wed/Sun for lunch.

King Edward VII) built a holiday home here, before demolishing it 17 years later. Between the chalets you snatch glimpses of the first of four lagoons that were excavated between the 1930s and 1950s – the shingle being used to make concrete for World War II airfields. Towards the end of the first lagoon, you reach **Snettisham Beach Sailing Club**, which was formed immediately prior to World War II. Chalets continue the length of the second lagoon, where the land to your right opens out into rough grassland and suaeda before admitting defeat at the estuary.

3 The path south now switches between firm shingle and concrete. Between the second and third lagoons, a trail enters from the left (east). Signposted to the RSPB car park, you will take this path on your return. For now continue south, perhaps pausing at **Rotary Hide** on your left (east), a fine spot from which to observe shorebirds on the mudflats to your right (west) or ducks and gulls on the lagoon. Opposite, the vestiges of a wooden jetty stutter westwards into **The Wash**. About ½ mile (0.8 km) further south, ignore for now the path (signposted 'circular walk') that bisects the third and fourth lagoons (you will return along this, however). Instead, continue south along the western flank of the fourth lagoon.

4 As you near the end of the fourth lagoon, where the **Shore Hide** may entice you to your left (east), shingle heath and suaeda stretch out in front of you. If you have coincided your visit with a 'shorebird spectacular' (page 82), head over to the benches by the shoreline to your right (west). When you have had your fill of flocks of waders hurtling overhead, follow the fenceline along a broad stony track as it rounds the southern tip of this final lagoon. Here there is a brand new hide built after the last one was destroyed by a tidal surge in 2013. On spring tides, the waders roost here. Continue north along the shingle path along the east side of the final lagoon.

5 After ½ mile (0.8 km), the path veers left (west) between the final and third lagoons. You now rejoin the path you took on the way out, but this time head north to the end of the third lagoon.

6 Here follow the signpost to the RSPB car park, heading right (east) between the third and second lagoons. The often-muddy path then weaves between hawthorns as it tracks the east side of the second lagoon, reaching the **RSPB car park** after ⅔ mile (1.1 km).

7 Leave the car park north along the muddy road, reaching the tarmac **Beach Road** after ⅓ mile (0.5 km). Turn left (west) onto **Beach Road**, passing rough grassland to your right (north) and the caravan site to your left (south) until you return to **Beach Road car park**.

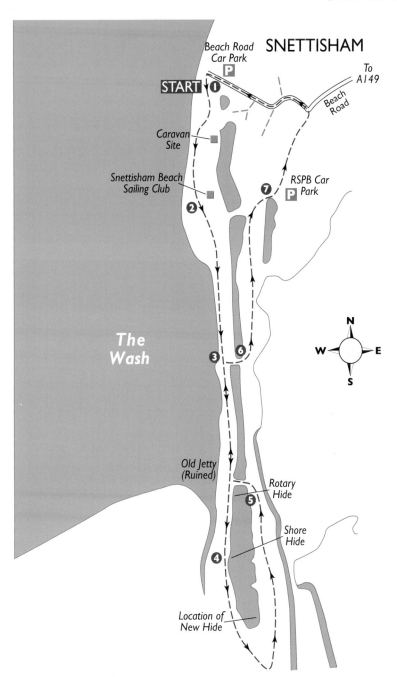

Beach Road
Car Park

P

SNETTISHAM

To
A149

START ❶

Beach
Road

Caravan
Site

Snettisham Beach
Sailing Club

RSPB Car
P Park

❼

❷

N
W E
S

The
Wash

❸ ❻

Old Jetty
(Ruined)

Rotary
Hide

❺

Shore
Hide

❹

Location of
New Hide

What to look out for –

Shorebird spectacular

Snettisham is famed for its high-tide shorebird spectacle. Particularly on a spring tide (for which see ⊕ rspb.org.uk/snettisham), incoming salty waters smother the estuarine mud before inundating the saltmarsh, depriving tens of thousands of waders of safe, dry terrain on which to roost.

And so the air starts to bulge with birds and their cries.

Oystercatchers take to the skies, turnstones quip, dunlins wheeze and redshanks yelp. Best of all, knot fly up en masse and billow through the air, alternately flashing silver and white to bewilder would-be predators before whooshing astonishingly low over our scalps to whirl down onto the adjacent lagoon. Once on dry land, each species keeps to its own. Knot take the lower shingle, oystercatcher linger higher up the bank, dunlin are relegated to the island. The knot in particular cram so close together that 20,000 birds merge into molten mercury.

18 Sandringham and Dersingham Bog

4¹⁄₃ **miles / 7 km**

The route ventures through woodland and heathland, and even tiptoes along the fringe of Dersingham Bog, a very special National Nature Reserve. Much of the walk traverses Sandringham Country Park, which forms part of the 20,000-acre Sandringham Estate, which has served as the private home of four generations of British monarchs since 1862. The Country Park has been planted with a mosaic of deciduous and evergreen trees. Corsican and Scots pines dominate, but they are complemented by oak, chestnut and birch. The blend provides habitat suitable for a range of wildlife, notably birds such as siskin, firecrest and crossbill.

Dersingham Bog is East Anglia's finest example of acid valley mire, and complements its soggy, mossy terrain with lowland heathland favoured by woodlark, stonechat and common lizard. As large car parks at Sandringham attest, this area can get busy in summer – making winter the perfect season for a tranquil wander!

The Walk

❶ As you park your car, listen for the high-pitched song of both goldcrest and the even more beautiful, and much scarcer, firecrest. The two species share the title of Britain's smallest bird, each weighing barely more than

The Facts

winter

Terrain Woodland trails (occasionally muddy), country lanes, sandy tracks and a boardwalk.

Map OS Explorer 250 Norfolk Coast West.

Starting point Car park at the Sandringham Estate visitor centre, which is west along a minor road off the B1440, south of Dersingham village (GR TF 689288).

How to get there & parking Take the A149 north from King's Lynn. One-and-a-half miles (2.4 km) after the junction for Castle Rising, turn right (east) onto the B1439. Pass through West Newton then turn left (north) onto the B1440. After 1 mile (1.5 km), the visitor centre and car park is signposted left (west) along a minor road. **Sat Nav:** PE35 6EH.

Refreshments At the visitor centre, Sandringham Café and Restaurant is open 09h30–17h30 daily except Christmas Day and Good Friday ⊕ sandringhamcafe.co.uk.

a 20p coin. Head south from the car park, turning right at a large wooden sculpture of a squirrel. Follow the path right, past a broad grassy 'fairway', towards a playground that is guarded by another wooden sculpture (this time, a bear). At the playground, take the right fork. You are now on **Princess's Drive**, which you will follow until you reach the public road at step 4.

2 The attractive woodland abounds with birds, from coal tit and treecreeper to nuthatch and chaffinch. In the first section, Scots pines rise steeply above a spartan understorey. After 250 yards, **Princess's Drive** becomes a private road that sweeps left as it enters deciduous woodland with scattered open areas. The road arcs right then left through **Jocelyn's Wood**, passing between towering rhododendrons which offer tempting climbing opportunities for young explorers.

3 After walking through such sylvan delights, it comes as a shock to find, on your left, the same broad grassy ride that you noticed on your approach to the playground in step 1. **Princess's Drive** is now marked by yellow arrows – not that you need them given that the road is now more or less straight so your route is obvious. The branches of huge pine trees form a guard of honour over the road. To your right, a raised wooden platform offers views westwards towards **The Wash**, one of Britain's largest estuaries (see page 78).

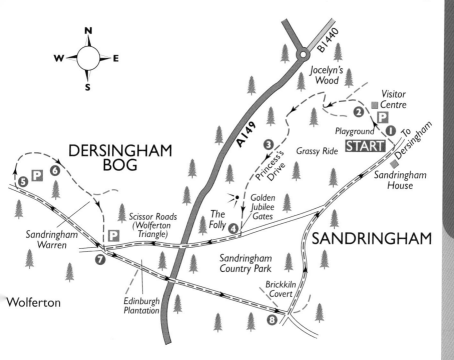

4 From this elevated viewpoint it is only 300 yards to the wrought-iron gates that celebrate The Queen's golden jubilee – and mark your arrival at a public road. Turn right (west) here, swiftly passing a house called **The Folly**. After ⅓ mile (0.5 km), you reach the A149. Cross this to take the minor road that lies almost opposite. This is the northern branch of what are known as the 'scissor roads' or 'Wolferton triangle'. Rhododendrons thickly flank this narrow road, which has long been visited by birdwatchers keen to see one of Britain's few remaining golden pheasants. At the crossroads, turn right past the 'scissors car park' and continue for ½ mile (0.75 km) to the tiny car park at **Dersingham Bog**.

5 On the north edge of the car park, follow the sandy track that threads between the rhododendrons. Turn left onto the 'clifftop stroll' (red markers) and follow it as it swings left then right along the top of a cliff. As the path swoops east it grants excellent views over the heather-rich plain of **Dersingham Bog** below. Where the 'clifftop stroll' meets the 'heathland ramble' (blue markers), walk down the wooden steps towards the bog.

6 A short boardwalk enables you to get a close view of the bog. See if you can spot small carnivorous plants named sundew in the wetter areas.

winter

Alternatively, listen out for a woodlark singing in the late-winter sun. Then rejoin the 'heathland ramble' and continue east across **Sandringham Warren**, bearing right at the fork to follow the blue signposts through birch scrub to reach the 'scissors car park'.

7 This brings you back to the crossroads on the 'scissors roads'. At the Give Way sign, go straight over to take the southern branch east towards the A149, with **Edinburgh Plantation** to your left (north). Carefully cross the main road, and continue walking east along the broad grassy verges flanking the minor road. This bisects **Folly Covert**, a tall mixed forest, with birch trees and bracken closest to the road and a pine plantation beyond. This is a good area to see finches such as redpoll and siskin.

8 After ²/₃ mile (1 km), you reach a crossroads by two lovely gatehouses, where you turn left (north). Walk along the road verge, past **Brickkiln Covert** on your left (west), for ¹/₃ mile (0.5 km) until you reach another road junction at a wide grassy area. On the opposite side of the road is a yellow trail marker. Cross the road to follow this path, which is joined by a blue trail as it proceeds north-east along **Scotch Belt**, parallel with the road about 40 yards to your right (east). Follow the path for ½ mile (0.8 km) to the visitor centre and car park.

What to look out for –

Golden Jubilee Gates

The Armed Forces presented Her Majesty The Queen with the pair of Golden Jubilee Gates to mark the 50th anniversary of her ascent to the throne in 2002. Sturdy structures, the gates are painted in black and gold, and have inscribed both relevant years (1952 and 2002). They mark the southern end of Princess's Drive, which provides the route for much of this walk.

19 Strumpshaw Fen and Buckenham Carrs

5 miles / 8 km

Aglorious winter's walk, comprising two loops through secret Broadland. Investigate a fenland nature reserve over which marsh harriers quarter, looking for voles, and through which otters pour. Stroll along country lanes through quiet farmland and beside damp carr woodland. Wander under big skies past grazing marshes resounding with the cries of ducks, geese and lapwings. And gawp at the mesmerising spectacle of tens of thousands of rooks and jackdaws swirling in the darkening sky before finding a safe spot to spend the night. Should you wish to enjoy the latter spectacle, and I strongly recommend that you do, you need to time your walk to arrive at Buckenham railway station an hour before dusk, and then bring a torch in preparation for completing the final stretch in the dark.

One note of caution: part of the riverside trail at RSPB Strumpshaw Fen occasionally floods in winter so, if notably high tides are forecast, call the reserve on ☎ 01603 715191 before you visit to check it is open.

The Facts

winter

Terrain Muddy paths and narrow country lanes, with one uphill section. Rubber boots recommended.

Map OS Explorer OL40 The Broads.

Starting point RSPB Strumpshaw Fen reserve car park, Low Road, Strumpshaw (GR TG 341066).

How to get there & parking Turn south off the A47 at the Brundall roundabout (by a Shell garage), following signs for Brundall. Follow Cucumber Lane south then, at the T junction, turn left (east) along The Street. Follow this all the way through Brundall, at which point you are on Strumpshaw Road. At the staggered five-way junction, turn right then immediately right again into Low Road, following signs for the RSPB reserve. Continue along Low Road for ½ mile (0.8km) to RSPB Strumpshaw Fen car park. **Sat Nav:** NR13 4HS.

Refreshments Hot drinks and cakes are available at the RSPB Strumpshaw Fen visitor centre during opening hours. ⊕ rspb.org.uk/reserves-and-events/reserves-a-z/strumpshaw-fen/. In Brundall, try East Hills Café Bistro ⊕ east-hills.co.uk; open 09h30–16h30 daily plus dinner Thu–Sat.

The Walk

❶ From the reserve car park, take the cut-through to the reserve entrance gate. Cross the railway line, pass the toilet block and arrive at the visitor centre. If you are not an RSPB member, please buy a permit here to access the reserve trails. Have a look at the open broad by the visitor centre; otters are sometimes seen or a strident 'cheeeeek' will herald an eye-searingly neon flypast from a kingfisher. Then follow the **Fen Trail** south from beside the visitor centre, proceeding clockwise. The path starts in woodland, with a pond-dipping area to your right.

❷ As you emerge from the wood, ignore Woodland Trail, which heads straight on, instead turning right (south-west) to continue along **Fen Trail**. To your right (north) is carr woodland, to your left (south) rough grassland over which a barn owl may float ethereally. After 300 yards, a side path leads right (north) to **Fen Hide**. This makes a pleasant diversion, offering a fine chance of seeing Chinese water deer, otter and marsh harrier. Return

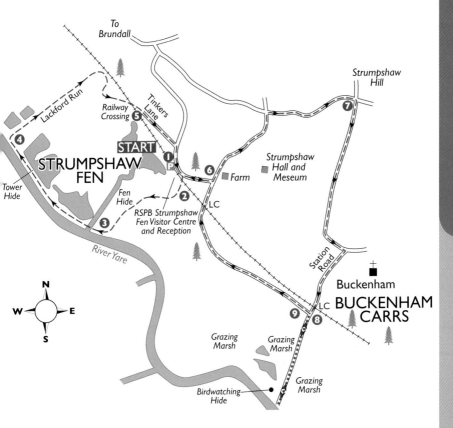

to the Fen Trail and continue south-west for 150 yards to the bank of the **River Yare** (pronounced 'yarr').

3 Turn right here, following **Fen Trail** along the east side of the river. This stretch can be muddy (and occasionally inundated on very high tides). Great crested grebes swim on the river, while reed buntings and Cetti's warblers inhabit the scrubby fen and reedbeds to your right (north). After ½ mile (0.8 km) you reach **Tower Hide** on your right (east) which offers stunning views over broad, fen and reedbed – usually complete with various ducks and the odd marsh harrier.

4 Continuing along the **Fen Trail**, the path swings perpendicular to the right (north-east) along what is known locally as the **Lackford Run**. This path passes through fen and reedbed for ½ mile (0.8 km) until it nears the railway line and jinks south-east. After 300 yards, cross the railway line to join a public footpath at **Tinkers Lane**.

5 Passing a large house on the left, continue along **Tinkers Lane** south-east until your feet hit concrete at **Low Road**. Turn right and walk south along **Low Road**, past the **RSPB car park** (where you started the walk), then continue east until you reach a T junction at a farm.

6 Turn left here (north-east) and walk gently uphill for ⅓ mile (0.6 km), past the entrance to the **Steam Museum** at **Strumpshaw Hall**, to reach a crossroads. Turn right (east), along **Stone Road**, walking for ½ mile (0.8 km) to a staggered crossroads at **Strumpshaw Hill**.

7 As this name suggests, you are now at the highest point of the walk, with the **Yare Valley** below. Then turn right, heading south along the continuation of Stone Road, which runs through arable fields. After ⅔ mile (1.1 km), the road bears sharply left. Take the next right along **Station Road**, signposted to Buckenham railway station. To your left, and somewhat less mobile than the corvids, is the church of **Buckenham**, beyond which is the woodland of **Buckenham Carrs**. At this point, should you be walking in late afternoon, you may start to notice what looks like a black oil slick spreading across a field. This is the pre-roost gathering of rooks and jackdaws. Descend **Station Road** to reach **Buckenham station**.

8 If you have a bit of time on your hands and fancy a short extension to the walk, cross over the railway line and walk straight on for 400 yards to the **River Yare**, then return. Grazing marshes on both sides are filled with birds – ducks such as wigeon and teal, lapwings, golden plovers and the odd hungry peregrine – and mammals, notably Chinese water deer. If you plan to watch the jackdaws and rooks swirl their way to roost in Buckenham Carrs, find a suitable vantage point near the station and look east. You may need to stay later than you expect, for the most impressive aerial shenanigans unfold when it is almost dark. When the curtain falls on the avian show, cross the railway line south.

9 Turn right (north-west) immediately and walk along the road past a few houses, fields and woodland for ⅔ mile (1.2 km) to cross the railway line at a staffed level crossing. Barely 150 yards on, turn left at the junction by the farm buildings and walk the residual 400 yards back to the reserve car park.

What to look out for –

Crow country

Long winter nights are all about sleeping, for birds as well as people. While humans tend to 'roost' alone or in pairs, many species congregate in large numbers to doze away the darkness. At the segue between night and day, such mass dormitories offer scintillating sights. Perhaps nowhere is better to experience these than Norfolk's Broadland.

Buckenham railway station platform is an unorthodox location from which to savour a remarkable natural spectacle: a pre-roost crowd of perhaps 40,000 jackdaws and rooks. Protagonists in nature writer Mark Cocker's enchanting book *Crow Country*, 'corvids' stream in from the gloom to gather in station-side fields and on telegraph wires. As the remaining light dissipates, the entire cacophony of corvids rises and cascades towards the night's arboreal abode in nearby Buckenham Carrs.

20 *Santon Downham*

3¼ miles / 5.25 km

Straddling both Norfolk and Suffolk, the Brecks are Britain's answer to the steppes of Mongolia: largely dry, sandy and arid lands with their own (peculiarly warm) microclimate. This Breckland walk takes in the Little Ouse River (where otters are regularly seen), mature pine forest, damp alder carr woodland, and the Brecks' unique sandy dune heathland. In late winter, snowdrops smother the ground with white. This is also the best remaining site in East Anglia for the rapidly declining lesser spotted woodpecker, which is most readily seen in late winter.

The Walk

1 Leave the car park at its far end (east), along the road (which also serves as **St Edmund Way**) and immediately pause to engage in a medieval mystery. The car park and surrounding grassland was the site of the village of **Santon**, which was occupied from at least 1086 until around 1670, when a series of sandstorms drove away the last remaining inhabitants. Low mounds are all that remain of the village, but the roughly square moat is relatively easy to see. Some archaeologists think that the moat marks the site of a manor house that was owned by the monks of Thetford Priory. Continue east along the road to reach the tiny **All Saints Church**, with its unusual octagonal tower.

The Facts

Terrain A combination of muddy paths; new, hard-surfaced footpaths; and the odd sandy stretch. Rubber boots advisable as the odd area can get boggy.

Map OS Explorer 229 Thetford Forest in The Brecks.

Starting point St Helen's picnic site car park (GR TL 826873), north-east of Santon Downham village.

How to get there & parking Access is from the A134 Thetford—Mundford road. Leave the A11 at Thetford, heading north-west from the roundabout along the A134 for about 3¾ miles (6 km), where you take the first turn on the left (west). (If you get to the sign for Grime's Graves, you have gone too far.) Continue along this minor road, through forest, for 1¼ miles (2 km). Just after the level crossing, turn left (east) to the car park at St Helen's picnic site. **Sat Nav:** IP27 0TT.

Refreshments Unfortunately, there is nothing nearby. Your best bet is to go to the towns of Brandon or Thetford.

2 Pass beyond the church and, just before a cottage, follow the signposted 'circular walk' path under the railway line. The path forks immediately at a large, isolated tree; take the right branch. A few yards on, head straight across at the crossroads, following the black arrow in a yellow circle rather than the yellow arrow on a blue circle that marks **St Edmund Way**.

3 You are now walking through a **Forestry Commission pine plantation**. Listen out for finches such as siskin and crossbill, plus typical woodland birds such as great spotted woodpecker and coal tit. At the first crossroads, turn left (north). At the second crossroads, turn left (west) to join the Forestry Commission **'orange walk'**. When you reach another crossroads, turn right (north). At the next crossroads (the fourth in this step of the walk), turn left. Continue straight on along a broad woodland ride, passing a smattering of rhododendrons on your left (south).

4 After just under ½ mile (0.7 km), the forest cedes to short grassland more typical of the **Brecks**. At a road lined with beech trees, turn left (south-west). After 50 yards, just before the level crossing, enter the car park to your right (west). Follow the path at the far end of the car park, which leads into a lovely area of sandy ground with stunted vegetation.

winter

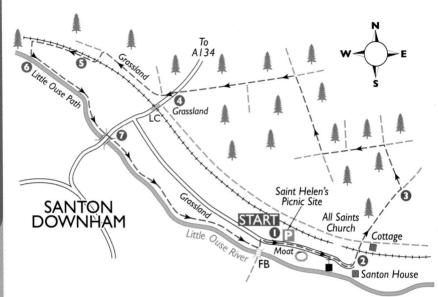

The habitat is sensitive here, with rare plant species, so keep to the path. If you have a dog, please keep it on a lead to avoid disturbing woodlark, a rare ground-nesting bird that breeds as early as February. When you reach a totem-pole-like structure, turn left (south) through the railway underpass, then turn right (west-north-west) to walk parallel to the railway. To your left is an area of damp ground with sedges, often grazed by longhorn cattle.

5 You soon come to an area of damp coppiced woodland on your left. Continue until the trees thin out, then choose a suitably dry area to cross the 50 yards left (south) to the northern bank of the **Little Ouse River**. There is no permanent path here, so it is a matter of selecting a sensible route.

6 You are now on a new hard-surface path, the **Little Ouse Path**, that borders the river. This is a good area for lesser spotted woodpecker. You may also see little grebe, mandarin and even water rail. Walk left (south-east) along the north side of the river. Scan ahead for otter. After ¹/₃ mile, cross the road bridge and go down the steps on the other side.

7 Continue flanking the river for ²/₃ mile until you draw level with a footbridge. Spend a while scanning the river east of here, which is another favoured area for otter. Then walk left (north), away from the bridge, to rejoin the car park which is a mere 50 yards away.

What to look out for –

Otter

The **Little Ouse River** has become a reliable place to see otters. This much-loved animal is enjoying a resurgence thanks to our increasingly clean waterways. To give yourself the best chance to see one, visit early in the morning, wear subdued clothing and keep noise to a minimum. Telltale signs include panicking little grebes or moorhens, or a v-shaped furrow (the otter itself) ploughing through the water. Fortune rewards the observant – and patient!

OTHER TITLES FROM COUNTRYSIDE BOOKS

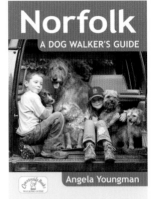
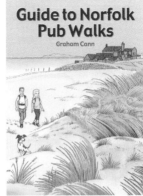
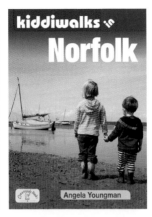

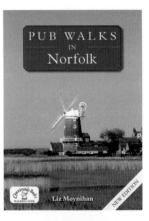

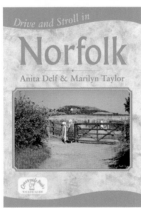

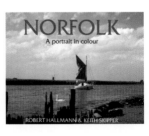

To see the full range of books by Countryside Books please visit
www.countrysidebooks.co.uk

Follow us on   @CountrysideBooks